GROW YOUR SPIRITUAL BUSINESS

HOW TO BUILD A BUSINESS
IN THE INTERNET AGE

CINDY GRIFFITH AND LISA K. PhD

FINDHORN PRESS

GROW YOUR SPIRITUAL BUSINESS

HOW TO BUILD A BUSINESS IN THE INTERNET AGE

CINDY GRIFFITH AND LISA K. PHD

FINDHORN PRESS

Published in 2015 by Findhorn Press, Scotland

ISBN 978-1-84409-674-9

Edited by Michael Hawkins
Cover design by Richard Crookes
Interior design by Damian Keenan
Printed and bound in the USA

Published by
Findhorn Press
117-121 High Street,
Forres IV36 1AB,
Scotland, UK

t +44 (0)1309 690582
f +44 (0)131 777 2711
e info@findhornpress.com
www.findhornpress.com

CONTENTS

CHAPTER ONE

Introduction

• • • • • • • • • • • • • • • •

Your classes are done, your certificate is in hand, and your teacher says you are ready. Congratulations, you are on the cusp of starting your spiritual business! So now what? Perhaps you already have a spiritual business that needs help attracting clients? Maybe you are really good at a particular healing modality or other type of spiritual business but have no business training? No worries, you can still learn how to run a spiritual business successfully.

This book was written to give you specific and proven steps that will ensure your new enterprise takes off from the very start with its spiritual focus and integrity intact.

A strong and profitable business does not mean throwing out your spirituality. *Grow Your Spiritual Business* will help you evaluate or reevaluate your business, prices, and marketing, while you take a professional approach and maintain your spiritual outlook. Both of us who wrote this book come from traditional business backgrounds, which allow us to offer you practical, grounded advice without compromising the spiritual values that are important to any spiritual business.

Lisa has a strong fifteen-year background in information technology, marketing and sales, driving multimillions of dollars in revenue for corporations around the world, and now runs her own successful spiritual business as an author, speaker and seminar leader teaching people internationally how to develop their intuition.

Cindy has run a successful practice as a psychic and spiritual teacher for over twenty years, more recently as an author, and before that she managed a real estate office, was an independent contractor in real estate sales and a real estate appraiser. Together, we offer you over 35 years of marketing experience in a way that fits your spiritually focused business.

HOW TO GET THE MOST OUT OF THIS BOOK

Grow Your Spiritual Business is designed in a way to maximize its usefulness to the spiritual business entrepreneur. You may find that some ideas are restated in different chapters, but this is purposeful. *Grow Your Spiritual Business* is organized so that you do not need to read it cover to cover — you can go directly to the chapters or sections that relate to what you need right now for your business.

Both Lisa and Cindy offer different but complementary views and advice, with examples from real life. Each chapter also includes **Spiritual Business Tips.** In these you'll receive the benefit of two experienced and successful spiritual business women who mentor you through the start, or advancement, of your own spiritual enterprise!

The best way to get the most from *Grow Your Spiritual Business* is by using the Table of Contents. Some of you who already have a spiritual business up and running may only need help in certain areas. Although you might benefit from reevaluating your business by starting in Chapter 1, you can instead look at the Table of Contents and go straight to the topic you need help in.

Using Lisa's core marketing concept of "Attract, Resonate and Synergize," you may find you are at different stages in your business and may only want to read the relevant chapters. For this reason, some core concepts are reiterated across chapters.

For those who are just starting out we recommend you read *Grow Your Spiritual Business* from the beginning. Starting with Chapter 2, *Exploring Your Passion*, will save you a lot of time and money! As we will demonstrate, it is your attitude that makes a business spiritual, and knowing your business identity is key in understanding how to market it successfully.

You may find that not all the topics in *Grow Your Spiritual Business* will apply to your business right away. In that case, we suggest you highlight suggestions you might want to try later, as your business grows. Also, you might not agree with every piece of advice, so take what you need and ignore what you don't. You will find that even Lisa and Cindy do things differently, which is another strength of *Grow Your Spiritual Business*, in that it offers two different perspectives on what works for developing a spiritual business.

As you read the chapters that follow, you'll know if it is Lisa or Cindy speaking by the use of different typefaces. In addition, Cindy's name will be marked by a slightly lighter shade of grey.

WHAT MAKES A BUSINESS SPIRITUAL?

The world is changing. More people than ever want to evolve both personally and spiritually. Everyone wants to live a better life and cruise through it with happiness and fulfillment. Maybe you have ideas for a business that you think will help. Maybe you've been thinking of venturing out on your own, following your inner urgings to do something more with your life. You feel that Spirit has put you on this earth to do more, to help others, and to make a difference. Or perhaps you've found a way to make your heart and spirit sing and you wish to make a career out of following that passion so you can share it with others.

There are many reasons why we are called to make a career change to do something more meaningful, with deeper spiritual value, so we can share those values with others. Whatever your reason, a spiritual business is a business that has spirituality at its core. The Oxford English Dictionary defines spiritual as "of, relating to, or affecting the human spirit or soul as opposed to material or physical things." Spiritual businesses are often inspired in those who have had their own spiritual journey or transformation and wish to help others do the same. Perhaps this is you? A spiritual business aims to rejuvenate, uplift, heal, inspire, comfort, and transform others, and will do the same for those running the business.

What makes your business *spiritual* is how you approach it. You bring your own spirituality to your business. Many modalities can be classified as a spiritual business. Just a few are energy healer, intuitive/psychic reader, yoga instructor, acupuncturist, massage therapist, herbalist, naturopath, life coach, spiritual teacher, etc.

You can see by these examples that spiritual businesses do not necessarily need to involve metaphysical practices — the spiritual part is what you as the practitioner bring to your business. You may be guided to be more spiritual in your business as a counselor, a nutritionist, a doctor, a teacher, or even a lawyer or accountant.

Most spiritual businesses fall into three categories of service: to motivate and inspire, to bring about life improvement, or to heal. Your business may overlap these categories. As a teacher, Lisa helps people develop their intuition so they can improve their lives by receiving inner guidance and wisdom. This training helps them in all aspects of their lives, and falls under "life improvement."

Cindy's spiritual business is also in the life improvement category. She helps people by giving them psychic guidance and information to enhance their lives. Yet she also helps her clients in healing through her energetic evaluations. Some spiritual businesses in the "healing" category heal the body, through physical movement like yoga or tai chi, or they heal the mind through affirmations and positive thinking as in the Law of Attraction. Spiritual businesses in the inspiring and motivating category move people to positive actions such as mindfulness, offer reinvigorating philosophies such as the Dao and Zen Buddhism, or promote natural living concepts that benefit the body and mind.

Whatever spiritual business you wish to pursue, it will probably fall into at least one of those three categories. Ultimately, the end goal will be to assist others to improve physically, mentally, and spiritually. As mentioned above, spiritual businesses do not have to be based in metaphysical practices, they can offer any service to others that motivates and inspires, improves their lives, or heals. Even a lawyer or accountant is there to be of assistance. What you bring to your work spiritually, whether it is helping the common good or doing work that inspires other people, will make your business spiritual.

In serving others, it is important to remember that making money does not keep you yourself from serving others. In fact, if you don't make enough money, you can't serve others! To reach people who need your services you need a business that is thriving well enough to sustain both you and it. Without the funds to get your business going, to keep it running, and effectively market it in order to reach those who need your services, you won't be able to fulfill your mission.

A spiritual business is a business that has spirituality at its core. Having a business-like marketing approach will help you connect with people who are looking for your services and a strong business infrastructure will keep your business viable. To be successful in helping others, you need both. Although you may have some trepidation now about this business thing, you don't have to. By putting some simple steps in place, steps we will put forward in this book, you will quickly be on your way to having a strong business structure that can help you reach thousands of potential clients and still allow your business to remain spiritual at its core.

Cindy Griffith and Lisa K.
Skaneateles, NY and Briarcliff Manor, NY
October 2015

CHAPTER TWO

Exploring Your Passion

· · · · · · · · · · · · · · · ·

YOUR BUSINESS IDENTITY

LISA The most important thing in starting a business is to be clear on what your business is about and why you are passionate about it. Clarity is key in any business for getting you started and reaching your goals. Many people find it difficult to narrow down what kind of business to focus on, particularly the kind of service they'd like to offer. You may be tempted to promote all the skills, modalities, and knowledge you have in your spiritual business marketing, but don't do it! Why?

Because prospective clients will have trouble figuring out exactly what you do. If they have trouble figuring out what you do, they won't know why you are the one they need. Or they may like the services you offer, but when it comes to word-of-mouth marketing, they won't know what to say to spread the word about you.

I know this pitfall well, because early on my business was not focused. I offered Reiki, Integrated Energy Therapy, Crystal Resonance Therapy, Traditional Chinese Medical QiGong Healing, Angel Therapy®, Angel Card Readings and Mediumship, plus meditation, Automatic Angel Writing™, and Intuition/Psychic Development. A few years ago, I realized I was doing too much when I had a customer rave about me and say she was talking to a friend she wanted to refer to me but then she had trouble explaining to her what I do. Her friend never did connect with me.

Pick one thing you are passionate about, best at, and love to do the most, and then center your business on that. I chose to be a teacher specializing in intuition development because intuition is my strength in knowledge and skill plus it is the key to all the other practices I am certified in. Intuition is also something I love and am passionate about.

I still offer other services, but I promote and focus most of my business energy on teaching intuition development. I also speak, teach and write about intuition. People now know me as an intuition teacher and expert.

When you focus your business identity, it will be easier for you to share your message with the world of what you have to offer and how people can benefit from it and you. You can generate word-of-mouth referrals more easily when you have a clear message of what you do and the kind of people you do it for. My message is to teach regular people how to develop their intuition so it becomes powerful and useful.

In this way, your marketing becomes simple and reaches the people who want and need your services or products. You won't be wasting your time and money going after people who are not interested. Now, with technology, it's so much easier to get to people who are already primed and ready to engage in a business like yours. In future chapters we'll go over ways to use technology to specifically reach your target market.

First, clarify what your business identity is. When you can sum it up in one sentence, customers can find you because they'll know what they can get from you. Create a one-sentence description of who you are and what you do. My description is: "I help people develop their intuition so they can make it happen when they want, on what they want and get detailed information." It is the opening to what they call in business an "elevator pitch." That is, telling someone what you do in the time it takes for an elevator ride.

Getting back to the story of how one customer was confused explaining what I did, that is history. Just recently a customer referred someone to me who was very interested in learning how to develop their intuition. Based on my clear business identity, my customer could quickly tell the person all about me — what I do, what my background is, and then rave about my services. The referral called me right away and we clicked instantly — she loved what I had to offer and was ready to buy immediately. This is the value of having a clear business identity.

CINDY Lisa offers some great points on narrowing your focus so that your clients don't get confused. I find the concept of focus so important, especially when it comes to marketing. To be clear, you can market your other modalities, yet you must focus on your biggest strength and, as Lisa said, your passion. I choose to market as a Psychic and that is what you will find in large print on my marketing material. If I create a large sign for a psychic fair or a brochure, I will add a few more things that are related, but in a smaller print so as not to confuse people.

For example, "Psychic Readings" is the main service I feature, but in smaller print I may put: Tarot Readings, Spirit Guide Readings, Energetic Health Readings, and Tarot Numerology. You will notice that these are all forms of Psychic Readings!

All too often I see people listing everything they do without featuring the main service or paying attention to marketing for that particular audience. At a psychic fair, if you are a psychic *and* a yoga instructor, you probably don't need to put "Yoga Teacher" on your sign. But at a health expo, a place you'd want to promote your yoga business, put Yoga Instructor and your certifications on your sign. If it is an event where people would be interested in psychics too, you can always put a small sign or object on your table that reflects your psychic business, such as a business card or brochure.

It is hard to know what people do best when they put everything they do on their marketing material. Recently I was at an event sitting across from a lovely woman who listed many services on her sign. None of the services was highlighted as the featured service and because she listed so many, the print was so small I couldn't read it! Her sign was so confusing that I had to ask her what she was offering at the show. Alas, she wasn't able to clarify the chief service she was offering and I remained as confused.

Most spiritual practitioners do in fact offer more than one service. But listing every little thing, especially if they are all very different, can create a "Jack of all trades" effect that gives off a "master of none" impression. I of course do more than Psychic Readings. I am a teacher, author, and scholar. I don't want to limit myself to one modality, so for the different hats I wear I have created different brochures and signs. If I want to make a brochure on classes I am teaching, I choose a title that fits the class. I might use Metaphysics Teacher, Meditation Teacher, or Spiritual Development Teacher.

I may, or may not, display every brochure I have at a given event. More often I evaluate which brochure best fits the event and then I either display the secondary brochures in a less prominent place or keep them behind the table in case someone expresses interest.

This is not to say there isn't value in cross-promotion, but it has to be handled in a focused manner. For instance, I have a small graphic of the cover of my book on my Psychic Fair sign, and beneath, it says "Author of *Soul Soothers.*" It adds clout to be a published author, but the image is in the lower corner of the sign and not a prominent feature because I am chiefly promoting Psychic Readings. If you choose to cross-promote, it should be a conscious decision as you remain focused on the chief thing you are promoting that day.

What Are the Goals of My Spiritual Business?

LISA The focus of many spiritual businesses is to serve others, which is great, because businesses, whether spiritual or not, are most successful when they focus on service to others. A spiritual business aims to rejuvenate, uplift, heal, inspire, comfort and transform others. There are many ways your business can do this. Once you have chosen a focus for your business, stay true to its spiritual essence by remembering your own spiritual principles. Your business focus, that is, the service or product you offer to your customers, and sticking to spiritual principles, will support your business goals.

Spiritually focused business owners shun the Ego fearing it takes away from the spiritual aspect of what they do. While spiritually it is important to stay out of Ego, at the same time you need enough Ego to put yourself out there and be able to run your business as a business. You can use your Ego to help you believe in yourself and accomplish your goals.

With many of the clients I coach, their biggest fear is whether they are capable enough to start their own spiritual business. You may feel the same way. There is no "best" time to start your business, you just have to jump in and do it. The only way to jump in is to have the courage and belief in yourself that you can do it. You have to start small, and take baby steps toward a larger goal. You may feel that the big goal of starting a thriving business is daunting, but setting your sights on the big goal helps you take the smaller steps toward getting there.

Something inspired you to consider starting your own spiritual business, so draw on that inspiration. When your heart is driving you to serve others, you only need to believe in yourself and believe that you can do it.

When you set your business goal, create a plan that begins with a series of small steps and accomplishments toward that goal. Don't measure yourself against someone who is making it "big" and expect that right away. We seldom see the level of effort and time that has been invested to make a business "big."

You should also think about what you want to get out of your business and how that plays into your personal life. Owning your own business, being your own boss, can be extremely satisfying, but at the same time all the responsibility lies with you.

You probably won't be making millions of dollars with your spiritual business. In fact, you'll probably start out making less money than your current full-time job. If your goal is to be happier and serve others then always keep that in mind as you move forward.

What Does a Client Receive From Me?

SPIRITUAL BUSINESS TIP #1

Transformation is a major goal of customers looking for a spiritual business.

CINDY In order to market effectively, you must be able to express what benefits your customers will gain from your product or service. Here are five easy steps to figure out what your clients will receive from you. This is not just an exercise, it will provide the fodder for all your marketing material to come.

STEP 1: Take time to write down what it is you actually do. If you are a massage therapist, what types of massage do you offer? If you're a psychic, you might also offer Mediumship, Medical Intuitive Readings, and Intuitive Counseling.

STEP 2: Once you have your services clarified , then make a list of the top five benefits your clients can expect from each of these services. It is fine to take a look at other practitioners' marketing for their business when you do this. As a matter of fact, I recommend it! Without copying verbatim another's promotion, you may find a good way to word a benefit or identify a benefit you haven't considered. Also, your clients will most likely be reading other practitioners' promotional materials, comparison shopping, so you need to know what that material says.

Remember that the goal is to realistically represent yourself in a way that stands out from others in your profession. In business everyone has different strengths, so you must determine your uniqueness, your strong points. You can say you are good at what you do without appearing boastful or imitative, or speaking negatively about how a "rival" business works. There are enough clients for everyone — it's your job to make sure those clients know why they want you! For example, a psychic's benefits may be: 1. Empowerment, 2. Peace of Mind, 3. Confirmation, 4. Guidance for Better Health, 5. Practical Steps for Spiritual Growth.

STEP 3: Once you have your top five benefits from Step 2, write a short paragraph to explain more about each, no more than fifty words or so, in one or two sentences. For example: "By connecting with my intuition and guides, I offer you proven and practical techniques, meditations, and visualizations that assist and support you to take the next step in your spiritual growth." (31 words, 1 sentence)

STEP 4: Now write down what your client will experience or achieve from working with you. Some people find this difficult, but if you can't express what a client will gain, clients may not understand why they should want what you offer. If you are not sure, seek out someone else who practices your service, and schedule a session. Note what your hopes are for the session and then what you actually gained from it. It might be something practical, like pain relief, or maybe a more ethereal effect like peace of mind or insight.

To help you articulate this, now determine what issues you will be helping your client with and that will become the benefit clients will receive from you. For example: "During your Intuitive Counseling session you will experience a supportive environment along with practical advice and insights geared to assist and support you as you find your spiritual truths and put them into your daily life. You can ask questions about anything you encounter, including how best to handle situations such as speaking your truth as you develop stronger and more healthy boundaries with family, co-workers, and friends." (68 words, 2 sentences)

STEP 5: Using the same technique of writing about each one, now change the form. Write three to five short sentences or phrases, bullet-point style, about what the client will receive. For example, your four bullet points may be something like this:

- Experience a supportive environment.
- Create healthy boundaries.
- Integrate your spiritual lessons into daily life.
- Receive practical guidance.

You will notice that with each bullet point, I open with a verb. When creating bullets it is best to use the same grammatical structure for each point. It is also okay for your bullet to be a fragment, it does not have to be a complete sentence.

Lisa and I have found that transformation is a major goal of those looking for a spiritual business. Transformation has become a catch phrase or key word in marketing, so it is important to be clear in your marketing about how your client will be transformed by your product or service. You could repeat Steps 1-5, this time asking, *How is my client transformed by my service?*

Following these five steps will not only give you a good feeling of what you are offering; the benefits, and how your service transforms your client, it will create an "elevator pitch" for you to describe what you do when someone asks.

How Am I Different From Other Practitioners?

SPIRITUAL BUSINESS TIP #2

Your Unique Selling Point tells the perspective customer what makes you different from other practitioners.

LISA What is your USP (unique selling point)? This is what makes your service or product different from others who offer similar services. It is meant to encourage customers to buy from you. Everyone has a USP because we are all unique: no one else is like you; no one else has the same experiences or knowledge you do. The trick is to figure out how your uniqueness brings value to your service or product.

Your uniqueness may lie in a transformational life experience you had that now makes you uniquely qualified to be the best provider for your service or product. For example, perhaps you found a way to solve a chronic health issue after years of seeking a fix, or you've been through a traumatic experience that led you to discover a spiritual path that changed your life and you now want to share that path with others.

Or you might discover your unique selling point from what others tell you. I've had many people tell me that the reason why they came to me is because I seem like a very grounded person due to my background in engineering and science. They felt they could relate to me because I wasn't "woo-woo" and I seemed like a normal person with my corporate background. They particularly liked my scientific approach to psychic and intuitive development. Having degrees in science and engineering gives me credibility in this area. I realized after I'd been told this over and over again that this attribute is my USP. It is the reason why people choose me over my competition.

You can also discover your USP just by listening to what people say to you. It is important to listen to praise. Many spiritually based business owners tend to be modest, and if you are like me, shut out hearing the complimentary words from people you have worked with. First, know that you deserve the praise! It is fine to acknowledge it, and when you do the Universe will send you more people who love what you do.

Listen to the kind words people give you, for they reflect what makes you different, what makes you stand out among others. It is not trumping yourself over others, it is simply recognizing that you offer people benefits they appreciate and like.

Your unique selling point may be your life story, or the story of how you got here, what you gained, what you learned, or how life became better for you. Everyone's story is unique, and so is yours. It may be the turning point in your life, or perhaps a life-changing epiphany. Or, like me, it could have been just an accumulation of knowledge that led to a new approach that others had not done before.

Yet another USP may be what you've done for other people and the successes they've had because of your services. This is not only proof that your service or product works, it also makes you stand out among the crowd.

SPIRITUAL BUSINESS TIP #3

The world doesn't need another spiritual practitioner; the world needs you.

CINDY The truth is that the world does not need another spiritual practitioner; the world needs you and what *you* bring into your chosen profession. If a client wants to find a new massage therapist, how will she know you are different than the other ten massage therapists she'll find looking online. It will be your marketing and presentation that helps the prospective client decide between you and the other practitioners.

To succeed in marketing in a way that stands out, make sure your marketing includes what makes you different as well as what you do and what benefits your clients will receive.

Knowing how you are different from other practitioners in your area is key to your marketing. This is why looking at other practitioners' promotion information is so important. Consider what you, as an individual, can offer that others in your field don't. Maybe it is your compassionate attitude or being a better than average listener. Maybe you have learned a technique and then added your own touch to it. What benefit can you bring the client above what the technique offers? Have you perhaps combined more than one technique in a way that others have not?

Here are some examples of things that may separate you from others in your modality. Maybe you:

- Offer a follow-up consultation for free or at a reduced price.
- Offer recordings of your sessions.
- Provide tips for better living in a PDF or on your website.
- Have extra training.
- Are known for your compassion, no-nonsense approach, easy-to-understand instructions, shooting from the hip, etc.
- Focus on a holistic approach.
- Offer weekend hours.
- Offer discounts for Military or those on disability.
- Combine two modalities where most others only use one.

The possibilities are as endless as you are unique!

Once you figure out how you are different, make short sentences for each or put them all into a 50-word paragraph. Like the 5 steps you followed earlier, you will use your bullet points or your paragraph in your marketing material and to help you be able to describe what you do when someone asks. Believe me, someone will ask and you want to be ready with a short answer!

At this stage of evaluating your business, visit other practitioners and experience what they offer. Pay the practitioner his or her full fee; don't barter. Get the full experience. Bartering may be cheaper, but you rarely get the same treatment as the paying client. By knowing what others offer, not only in the quality of their service, but in atmosphere, ease of booking an appointment, professionalism, value, etc., you gain a better understanding of what makes your service unique. You'll also know who to refer your clients to if you are not the best one to fulfill their needs.

For example, I am not a medium, so I need to know someone to refer people to who are looking for a medium. Also, I am not great at finding lost objects. I send my client with lost objects to another psychic who is better at it. I have rarely found that I have lost a client by doing so. Actually, referring a client to someone else when I was not the best person to answer his or her question has created goodwill, and the client will come again when his or her need matches what I offer.

While contemplating other practitioners, avoid looking at them as competition. Each practitioner has unique strengths. When you are not afraid to refer someone else, it says to the client, "I want what is best for you, not my bottom line." It also sends the message to the universe that you feel secure that there is enough work to go around. Some of my best referrals have come from other practitioners who know I offer something they don't.

Part of the definition of a spiritual business is that it is inclusive, working toward creating a community where those who are spiritually minded can connect. When you work together with other practitioners through referrals and events, you create a spiritual network that answers a multitude of needs. If you are afraid to recommend other practitioners, clients will feel your fear and competitive attitude, while sensing that you are not walking your talk.

LISA Cindy is so right about being non-competitive. One of the things I love about being an Angel Reader is that many of those in the "angel" community are less competitive and that may be because of our teacher. My teacher once said to us, "There are seven billion people in the world, there are enough customers to go around."

I love that! I have worked with my colleagues, including Cindy, on a very collaborative basis that is deeply spiritual and we all benefit from that. The benefits are both material from our collaboration and spiritual as good souls.

How Is My Business Perceived in My Area?

CINDY Researching your business is a must for success. Whether you are just getting started or reevaluating your spiritual business, there are important questions to ask yourself. A great spiritual business idea can struggle to find its identity and you can waste time and money because you did not do enough research before you created your business cards.

For example, although it may sound silly, make sure there is a demand for your service. Are you the only iridologist because no one else wanted to study that field or because three iridologists before you have not been able to educate people well enough to understand the benefit? Are there already four iridologists in a one-mile radius around your home? Competition or another's lack of success is not a reason to give up on your dream business, but it will require more marketing, educating, and networking.

Assuming you have done your research and know there is a demand for what you do; next explore how your field is perceived in your area. When

I lived near New York City, you might have thought that I could charge higher rates than in the small town in Central New York I live in now. Wrong. Psychics are more highly respected in Central New York and paid better! Yet classes are more highly valued downstate, and this is shown in students willing to pay more for a workshop in the New York metro area.

To find out how your business is perceived, look to see if there are other people doing what you want to do. But just because there is no one else in your field, it doesn't mean that your service is viewed poorly.

Here are some ways to determine how your business is perceived in your area:

1. Ask friends that have been in the spiritual circles longer than you if someone else has tried your spiritual business and how it went.
2. If the business didn't make it, ask your friend why she thinks the person didn't succeed.
3. Ask the kind of people you think would be prospective clients if they have heard of your type of business and whether they know its benefits.
4. Search online for businesses like yours in your area. For example: I would search for keywords – Psychic in Central New York or CNY.
5. Contact your local Chamber of Commerce. Ask if spiritual businesses like yours exist or if they did in the past. If they are no longer around, ask if they have any ideas why the businesses closed.

If you think your business is not well perceived, make sure it isn't your fear of going public. I used to be afraid to put "Psychic" on my door and so my door plaque read "Intuitive." People had no idea what it meant! If you are fearful of judgment, you will create that judgment.

Often a business fails because the practitioner isn't a good businessperson or didn't educate the public well enough. Whether your business is not well perceived or no one else is offering anything like you are offering, your first task will be to start educating your prospective clients on why your practice is valuable and why your service is worth their hard-earned cash.

Speaking at libraries is great for this, along with other events like wellness festivals, psychic fairs, and other lecture opportunities.

Shine the light on what you do and why someone might want to experience it. Offer a free talk or class at a local adult education center, health fair, psychic fair, or bookstore. Don't worry if no one shows up, the advertising of the event will introduce people to your topic. You may need to offer the same free talk three to six times before someone will show up.

Avoid turning your talk into a sales pitch; instead educate the attendees on what your practice is, what it can do, and why they might benefit.

This is not to say you should leave your marketing material at home. Save it until the end and hand it out after the attendees have had time to become comfortable with you, or put your marketing material in a packet along with some notes from your talk for them to take home. Everyone loves notes, and it never hurts to add a steep discount with a relatively short expiration date for the first session. I would avoid a free first session, as people tend not to take them seriously.

Other ways to increase awareness can be running ads that contain more about the modality and its benefits than about you. Writing blogs and articles are helpful to change perception. Again, avoid the sales pitch. If you are writing the article to shift the perception of your business, your article shouldn't be about you; it should be about your service and what the reader will gain from it.

Make sure your bio contains your qualifications, that you have a business, and includes a link to your website. We'll go over more of this in future chapters.

WHO ARE MY CLIENTS?
Demographics

> **SPIRITUAL BUSINESS TIP #4**
>
> Knowing your prospective clients is key to understanding why they are looking for your services or products.

LISA Knowing who your prospective clients are is key to understanding why they may be looking for your services or products. From this you will gain insight into how to market to them and let them know you are available to help. The prospective clients are called your "target market."

Let's start with your answering a few questions. What is it that you do for others? For example, I teach people how to develop their intuition.

The next question you need to ask yourself is, who would be interested in my service or product? This will define the people you want to reach in your market. You may be tempted to say everyone is interested in what you have to offer, but we all know that not everyone likes the same thing. That's okay! You want to narrow down the kind of person you want to reach.

Start by looking at your current customers and note their similar traits. What kinds of people attend your seminars? Who are your favorite customers? Look for common interests and personality traits. Which customers bring in most of your business?

If you don't have customers yet, look at similar businesses and see what kind of people frequent those businesses. You most likely have gone to those businesses yourself. Have you taken a seminar in the subject area of your business? What kinds of people attended the seminar?

In my business, I find most of the people who attend my seminars and intuition development groups are women over the age of 35; most of them are middle-aged and looking for more in life spiritually. The gentlemen who come to my seminars tend to be older and are often looking for more spiritually. They all have a belief in intuition and curiosity about the world. I love this group of customers; I truly enjoy being, teaching and working with them. We have a blast!

Now that you have a clearer idea of what your business identity is and who your potential customers are, you can go find them. Better yet, you can help make it easier for them to find you! The quicker you can connect to prospective clients, the faster your business can grow and you can attain the goals you're seeking.

To clarify, here are the kinds of things you can think about for the customer that would be attracted to your business. I have added after each one, as an example, my target customer characteristics in italics.

- Gender - *Female*
- Age range – years or categories such as teenagers, young adults, middle age, seniors, etc. – *35 years old and up*
- Personal interests – what do they like on Facebook? – *Spirituality, psychic development, New Age topics, self-improvement, self-help*
- Location – where do they live or work? – *My most active customers are currently in the New York Tri-State area, though online I reach people in the US, Canada, Australia, and the UK.*
- Household Income – *Over $30K*

- Education level - *Generally college educated*
- Lifestyle – *Many are retired or have older children, love to read, do retreats, enjoy learning about how to improve their lives, interested in eating healthy and living ecologically conscious lives.*

Once you know who your ideal customer is and who will most likely want to purchase your services or products, then you can go find them more easily.

SPIRITUAL BUSINESS TIP #5

Understanding your prospective clients is key to good marketing.

CINDY As Lisa said, know your clientele and demographics. If you are retired, enjoy a mature client, or have no patience with young adults, you may find that going into the henna-painting field may not be the best choice (unless you are in a community where henna is part of a spiritual ceremony). For my psychic business, my main clientele are women between the ages of 25 and 60. As I have aged, my demographic has shifted slightly. In the past twenty-plus years, my demographic has only become ten years older and the youngest has stayed the same.

Why do you need to know your demographic? Let's say I get an invitation to advertise in a program for the town's professional baseball club. I might want to decline, as the target audience would not be 25-to-60-year-old females. But the same ad in a baseball program for school-aged kids might work as the children's moms, probably ages 25–50, would see the ad.

What Are My Clients Looking For?

LISA Once you know who your customers are then you can assist them better by providing services and offerings that are perfect for what they want. This is key, since people buy what they want, not what they need. When you know the kind of people your customers are, the problems they want to solve, the desires they have, then you can better serve and connect with them.

CINDY Here, again, when trying to determine what your clients want, it is helpful to look at brochures and promotional material of other practitioners. Although you aren't going to copy what others have said, it is nonetheless helpful to get others' ideas to get you thinking. Also, it is helpful to ask friends and acquaintances what they are looking for in a practitioner. This is where social media comes in handy. For example, on your social network, ask the question, "What do you want to get out of your Reiki session?" or "What information would you want to know about a Massage Therapist before you go for a session?"

I have used social networking when I am trying to get a feel about how my clientele will respond to a new idea. I've been very happy with the results.

Once you understand what your clients want, then you can go about making sure that you provide those services and that your marketing material reflects what your clients are looking for. People want their hard-earned money to get them the results they desire. If you can assure prospective clients that you can deliver, while presenting yourself as a professional, you are much more likely to get their business.

WHAT IS MY IMAGE?

LISA Many times spiritually oriented people are shy and sensitive. They often feel strongly about being of service to others and shun anything that feels egocentric. Yet, when it comes to your business, people will want to get to know you. People relate better to people rather than a business name, and when they feel comfortable with you they are more likely to do business with you. If you are selling a service you personally provide, for example, healing, teaching, readings, etc., people want to know YOU.

How you present yourself is important in making people feel comfortable about trusting you and that you know what you're doing. Let's say you went to a doctor and she looked like she just rolled out of bed, hair tousled, and seemed like she'd had a little too much to drink the night before. You would not feel very comfortable going to that doctor for medical care.

The shyness of "putting myself out there" was something I needed to overcome for business. This particularly became clear when I needed a professional photograph taken of me (also called a headshot), listened to myself on the radio, or watched myself on a video. People want to see and hear you before they do business with you.

Although being in front of a video camera or on a podcast or radio is not necessary for a business, these tools help in building a relationship with your customers.

CINDY A prospective client will connect with the person rather than the service. If the client isn't comfortable with the practitioner, he or she won't come back. If customers deem the website or marketing as unprofessional, they won't come at all. A prospective client cannot connect with a blank slate. It is not egotistical to let people know who you are.

Because more and more people are turning to spiritual businesses, there are more and more spiritual businesses out there. The need for a professional image and good marketing so that you stand out has become even more important. Marketing is not "unspiritual" in itself. It is how you market that determines the level of spirituality.

What Name Will I Use?

LISA Choosing a name for your business is a very important first step that influences how your customers find you and relate to you. You'll want to pick a name that is easy for people to remember, easy to say, and easy to spell. It is important that your business name is relevant to who you are, especially if you are providing a personal service as a practitioner or a teacher. Some people use more than one name, or use separate names for the business and their own name for promotion. Having one name is easier for people to remember and also keeps all of your marketing material consistent.

Generally, if your business is a service that you yourself are providing, the name should reference your own name. If your name is hard for people to say, spell or remember, you can shorten it or use an alias. My last name is long and difficult for people to spell, say, or remember, so I only go by my first name and last initial, which is also my business brand name and is my "Doing Business As" (DBA) name. I've found this makes it much easier for people to identify and remember me.

Try not to use names that are too loosely related to what you do. "Angel Breath Starlight Whisper Services" is vague and difficult for people to remember. Instead use a short descriptive name. On the other hand, "Starlight Reiki Energy Healing" would be a good name for a business providing Reiki energy healing because it is very specific and people know right away what it is.

Also, aliases lack a feeling of authenticity and can make people feel you are trying to hide something. For example, Crystal Star may not be a good name for your business, unless your real name is Crystal Star. People want to relate to a person they can identify with, not a pseudonym.

CINDY We know a number of people who use aliases, and Lisa and I are not saying it is wrong to do so, only that you might want to think about how it sounds. For example, a friend was using the name Cougar Woman, as she was a shaman and had cougar as one of her totems. She couldn't understand why she kept getting young men asking her out on her social media page. For her, cougar was sacred — for the young guys, not so much!

I have another friend who is single, attractive, and lives on her own. She has chosen to use an alias so that a client can't look her up and come to her house uninvited. She chose to use only a first name and picked one that was simple, easy to remember, and didn't sound far out.

I have name recognition in my profession, and so when I married at forty, I chose to legally hyphenate my name. I continued to use Cindy Griffith for business because no one would have known who Cindy Bennett was. I didn't use Griffith-Bennett until I co-wrote my first book with my husband.

I have decided to go back to Griffith for all books I write in order to keep my original name recognition. My website used to be PsychicSupport.com, yet except for a logo I used occasionally, I did not feature it on my marketing material because it did not connect to my name. I recently changed my website to CindyGriffith.com as it is clearer, easily remembered, and directly connected.

When you know what type of business you are, you are ready to move forward with your spiritual business. Strong time management skills are vital if you want to accomplish everything necessary to be successful in your spiritual business and still have time to enjoy life. So, time management is where we will focus before moving on to picking a location for your spiritual business.

CHAPTER THREE

Getting Started

· · · · · · · · · · · · · · · ·

MASTERING TIME MANAGEMENT

LISA Many of my clients who want to start spiritual businesses are already working or are in another kind of business. A spiritual business often begins as a side interest that began from an inspiration. If you already have a full-time job, working to earn a living, or if you are a full-time mom, you are going to be very busy already! It is key to your success to know how to manage your time if you would like to start your own business. Don't feel you have to quit your job to start your spiritual business. You can start it slowly while you keep your "day job."

As an entrepreneur fully immersed in running your business, what you spend your time on is vital to keeping your business running. All small businesses require owners to be "chef, cook and bottle washer," which can be overwhelming. Whether starting a business while you are working another job or running your small business, the key will be time management.

CINDY In order to help you get the most productivity out of your valuable time, Lisa and I offer some time management tips. In the beginning, if you can't manage your time it will be frustrating to manage your business and keep the rest of your already busy life going. Time management doesn't have to be difficult. The following sections offer basic steps to get everything done without sacrificing your lifestyle.

Grounded Spirituality

SPIRITUAL BUSINESS TIP #6

Set aside "chunks" of time to work on your business marketing.

LISA Surprisingly, too much spirituality can unground you and take you away from the things you need to focus on to keep your business thriving. This can happen when people feel that if they are highly linear and systematic in their business thinking it will detract from their spirituality. But we are meant to be both spiritual and grounded at the same time.

There are times when you need to focus on your day-to-day business tasks that require more left-brain, logical thinking and then switch to your spiritual mode when you are actually practicing your spiritual craft, whether it be energy healing, intuitive readings, alternative medicine, or spiritual consulting.

Stay focused when you need to be, and focus on what you need to focus on. The best way to do this is to be disciplined enough to set time aside daily for your business tasks. A good way to help manage your busy schedule is to work in "chunks" of time.

First, turn off all distractions — even though it's hard, you can do it. Don't look at your email, close your email application; don't look at your social media; turn the ringer off on your phone; and, if possible, make sure the kids won't or can't bother you. Set a timer for 50 minutes and just work on one business task. After your 50 minutes is up you can take a 10-minute break to do whatever you want — go stretch, snack, look at your texts, check on the kids, etc.

But after that 10 minutes, set your timer again for another 50 minutes and work again solely on one business task. You'd be surprised how much you can get done. We often get very distracted and therefore it takes a long time to get anything finished.

Productive Multitasking

LISA Being an entrepreneur, which is what you are when you have your own business, is highly demanding of your time and focus. When you work for a company, as I did, in some ways it's actually easier to manage your time because you are generally assigned to do one thing, or one job.

As a lone businessperson you have to do so many different things, it's hard to get anything done. I could run and manage a multi-million dollar project with 100 people working for me when I was working in corporate, but when it came to my own business I was overwhelmed with so much to do.

Time just seemed to slip away from me. It felt like it took me years to move inches. Before I learned how to "chunk" my time, I tried to work on several things at once. It was hard to keep my focus on deadlines for several different major projects. I would change the projects, the due dates, and what I did each hour at will. It was almost too much freedom!

Once I chunked out my time and focused my energy on one project during that chunk of time and then another project in another chunk of time I was able to accomplish and complete many projects together. If you focus on one thing at a time per chunk you can get more done across many projects, rather than being random and scattered doing several projects all at once.

In your chunk of time, pick one thing you will work on out of the several projects you need to do, and focus only on that *one* thing. If you are a perfectionist, then try to stop at 90% of what you think is best, otherwise you'll have trouble completing things in a timely fashion. Most of the time, 90% is more than enough.

Set due dates for important stages of your projects. Then work towards those dates. When we work for ourselves we don't have fixed dates for completion. That can mean time whips by too quickly without our noticing it. To prevent that, pick dates when you want to accomplish certain milestones of your projects by and pick a date when you want the entire project completed. Then work toward those dates. You can adjust them later if you really need to.

I found that picking a date to teach a class and announcing it made me work harder to prepare for it. In this way I was able to create courses much more quickly. I also have recurring events I need to prepare for each month such as my intuition development group meeting and my radio show. These fixed events also force me to create a monthly newsletter email announcing the event details and also gets me to write an article to be included in my newsletter.

Also, finding a good place to work and concentrate is important, if you can do it. I have spent some of my summers dedicated to writing large projects, like this book. I found that the library of my alma mater, Columbia University, is a fantastic place to work and concentrate. It's quiet, and since everyone there is intensely focused, it makes for great work energy!

Here is a summary of how to get things done:

1. Chunk your time.
2. Shoot for 90% perfect rather than perfection.
3. Focus on one thing in your chunk time.
4. If you can, find a quiet place where you can focus and work.

CINDY I know Lisa's suggestions work because I use them. However, don't worry if you don't have a 50-minute chunk of time. If you have another full-time job or you are a stay-at-home mom, you may find that your lifestyle only gives you a 20-minute chunk of time before the kids get home or before bedtime. Do the best you can with the time you have. You will be amazed how much you can get done in whatever chunk of focused time you can manage.

Motivation

LISA Keep in mind what you are striving for, that is, what is your goal in having a spiritual business? Is it to serve others? If so, why? Focusing and staying grounded will keep you moving toward your goals and being more productive. It's important to remember your service to others. Also, when you stay true to being of service to others, your authenticity comes through and your business will automatically be more successful. Both people and the Universe respond to authenticity and being true to service.

It is easy to lose sight of why you started your business in the first place, because we all get caught up in life and compare ourselves to others. What you have to share with the world will match the very best customers and clients that are meant for you. We must remember that in our service to others there is no competition because we are all working toward the same goal: helping to make the world a better place. The Universe will respond by connecting you to the places, people, and things that are in alignment with your intentions, goals and motives.

In fact, if you are going into a spiritual business because it makes you feel important and better than other people, your business probably won't last. That's because your customers will sense the self-importance in your motives and will instinctively stay away.

By the same token, you should honor the cycle of giving and receiving, which is the natural process of energy flow in the Universe. If you give, you will and should receive, whether it is in the form of money, praise, or appreciation. Be accepting of this, and allow it to come to you, but don't let it expand your Ego. You receive with a "thank you" and your own appreciation of the gifts that have been bestowed upon you because of your service and giving to the world.

I always thank the people who give to me and I thank my angels and God for the cycle of energy that has brought me the good things, such as money and appreciation. Besides, appreciation and testimonials are great ways to spread the word that people are benefiting from what you offer and others may, too!

Schedule Time With Yourself

CINDY Another time management technique is to schedule repeated times on your calendar for specific jobs and then guard those times as sacred. Often we put time aside for the gym, meditation, or our kid's soccer game, but for business planning — not so much. For example, when I am writing, I often put aside Tuesday and Thursday mornings for it and then do my best not to schedule anything else. Given that I don't have a 'day job' or children to look after, I can put aside an entire morning.

You may decide that you will work on bookkeeping from 8 to 9 each Thursday, but not force yourself to work on Tuesday night during your favorite TV show. When I start a chunk of time, I know that first I will check my email and respond to clients, but I am careful to stay away from Facebook and other activities in which I tend to lose track of time. I then leave the house and go to the café because the distractions at the house are too tempting. There is always laundry, the phone, or the refrigerator just waiting for my attention.

Not everyone has the luxury of spending time at the local café or college library, so maybe close the door and put on your headset for your time chunk. I find if I put the time into my calendar for a few weeks in advance, it is easier to avoid scheduling other things to do during my sacred work time.

The important thing, like Lisa says, is to have chunks of time that you focus on one thing. Taking one project at a time is the smartest way to get a lot done without getting overwhelmed. Break down that big project into small, manageable steps. That is how we designed *Grow Your Spiritual Business*: it breaks down the sometimes overwhelming business of business into small manageable chunks. Done one step at a time, you will find that you have all the time you need to successfully run and market your spiritual business.

LISA Cindy makes some great suggestions here, especially when you don't have an alternate place to work that can help you focus. If you can find a café or a library I highly suggest it. I have found that writing in a college library is the best energetic space to focus and get a lot of concentrated work done. I wrote large sections of this book as well as my PhD in the libraries of my alma mater.

You may want to find a place that energetically suits your work style. Everyone is unique in what kind of environment they work best in. You may need to work where it is very quiet and others may need the buzz of an office-like environment or have music playing in the background. Find a place where you work best and schedule time for yourself there.

SETTING UP YOUR WORK SPACE

`CINDY`   Before you start marketing and letting people know you are open for business, the issue needs to be decided of where to set up shop and how clients will contact you for appointments, products, and more information. Here are some questions you might want to ask yourself.

- Do you want an office in your home or do you want to be in a professional building or New Age center with like-minded practitioners?
- Can your business, such as consulting or coaching, be done over the phone or do you need to meet with people face to face?
- Do you want people calling you on your home phone, a separate business phone, or would a cell phone or Internet phone number work best?

These are all things you need to decide before you spend money on a website, brochure, and business cards. Once you know where and how your clients will reach you, you still need to figure out what you are going to charge and how you will get paid. Don't worry, all that is in the next chapter. With a few decisions made, you can start the creative venture of designing that website and those brochures, flyers, postcards, and business cards.

A Clutter-Free Workspace

`CINDY`   Whether you choose to work out of your home or rent office space, it is important that your workspace be clutter-free, professional, and if at all possible, separated from family or office-mate foot traffic. Although I do most of my readings over the phone or at psychic fairs, I have people come to my home for readings. I live in Skaneateles, a quaint small town with a lake and lots of shopping and restaurants, so people like to come there for a reading and a day at the lake.

Although I don't clean the house as I would if my mother were coming, I make sure to straighten up. I give clients their reading in a room with a door that closes, to give a feeling of privacy. I used to have my reading room in the middle of the house, but then my husband could not come downstairs when I had clients. It works much better now that I have moved my office into a room with a door. I also recently purchased a "white noise" machine to further give the client privacy. I highly recommend one of these machines, which mask other sounds, if you are in a home where other people live or in an office with thin doors and walls.

I remember going to a psychic years ago, traveling over an hour to a remote area to see her. My friend had highly recommended her, but when we drove up to the littered yard, I wasn't so sure. The psychic came to the door in a ripped T-shirt, and we had to walk through her kitchen with dishes stacked up high in the sink to sit in her messy living room for the actual reading. Her family was hanging out within view during the reading. I was grossed out just being there. She may have been a great psychic, but all I remember is how uncomfortable I was. I never went back.

Now, I'm sure your place of business could never be that bad, but even a mildly cluttered space could be discouraging to a client. It is important to remember that objects, including paperwork, carry energy. Every knick-knack has its own energy and sometimes too many of them can confuse the space, especially if they are dusty or disorganized. You want your space to make the statement, *I care about you, my client, and the space we work in.* You do not want to make the statement, *I really don't have time for my business or for you.*

It isn't only clutter that affects your space. Every time you think negatively with thoughts like, *I am a bad person for not getting to my bills*, or *I don't have enough time,* that message energetically fills the room. Your client may not know exactly what the energy is, but they will feel a judgmental or confused energy when they walk in.

I have clients of all faiths and some of no faith, so I make sure the objects on my altar space by my reading table are multi-denominational, yet not overly religious or New Age-ish. I have mostly crystals in that space. I also have Ganesh, who is the reliever of obstacles, a meditating cat and dragon, and a little sign that has a picture on it of penguins that says, *Relax, God is in charge.*

I try to remember to dust that space, although no one is perfect — as I write this in the café, I make a note to myself to dust when I get back home! Lisa and I have included pictures of our work spaces for you to see.

Cindy's workspace.

Lisa's workspace.

WHERE TO WORK WITH CLIENTS

CINDY Working from home is not always practical, yet a full-time office is often not in the budget when you start out. A lot of your choices depend on your chosen modality. First decide if you can see your clients in person, over the phone, or both.

Questions to ask about a business with a home office are:
- Do I know my clients before they come for their session?
- Do I live in an accessible area?
- Is it legal or am I allowed to receive clients in my home?
- Do I have a clean and quiet space for my work?
- Do I have a space where no one will come in or near while I am with a client?
- Will other family members be okay with me having people in our home?
- Would I feel safe having a stranger in my home?
- Do I want to have the energy of strangers in my home?
- Can I get and afford extra insurance if necessary?

Questions to ask about a business in a traditional office are:
- Does my particular business require other practitioners?
- Do I have enough clients yet to be on my own or to pay for an office space?
- Do I need referrals from other practitioners?
- What are the costs associated with the office space, such as electricity, heating and cooling, and can I afford them?
- Are there adequate parking and bathroom facilities?

Once you answer these questions, you will have a better idea if you need to rent space somewhere or can have people come to your home.

Location, Location, Location

CINDY It is great if you find a beautiful, affordable office, but can and will people travel to it? I recently had a client ask about a spa she was starting. I happen to know the area, and it is not convenient. This is not to say the business couldn't flourish, but she was hoping to attract clients from an affluent nearby community. I flat-out asked her if she thought people from "affluent town" would think "small, not affluent town" for a luxurious spa experience. She paused for a moment and then said, "No." It was not the end of her business, yet her answer required that she rethink her marketing strategy. Her spa business could be quite successful, just maybe not with the clientele she was thinking of. People will travel quite a way for the best in the business, yet until you get known as such, you may want to consider having a location that is easy to get to!

LISA Some communities have a built-in customer base for your spiritual business. For example, Sedona, Arizona is known as a place where people go to look for spiritual activities and have a spiritual experience. Sedona has a built in spiritual community beause of this. Sometimes it is hard to find those communities where you live.

I have lived in my particular county for thirty years but it was only in the past eight that I discovered there were enclaves of spiritual businesses in certain towns. I hadn't looked for them before. What you can do is network and talk to other practitioners to see if they know of locations and businesses that cater to your kind of spiritual business.

Home Office Location

SPIRITUAL BUSINESS TIP #7

Before you set up your home office make sure your family
is really okay with having strangers in the house.

CINDY If you choose a home location, you will want to have some sort of insurance umbrella. Most homeowners' insurance policies will not cover a client if you do not have a legally set up business and the proper zoning. The requirements change from state to state, so check with your municipality and your insurance company.

You also want to make sure your family is okay with having strangers in the house. I have a friend who has a wonderful husband, very supportive of her and her business, but he is not comfortable with her having clients in the home. It is important to respect your family members. If they are resentful or angry with you having clients in the home and you do it anyway, your clients will feel that sentiment when they walk through the door.

There is also the safety issue. Yes, we can put all the protective golden light we can muster around the house, but still, if you don't know who is coming to your home, you could be inviting in someone who doesn't have your best interests at heart. Plus, people have energies that may not match your home. Most spiritual businesses, in one way or another, help people release their negativity and raise their energetic vibration.

Each time someone releases energy, the energy has to go somewhere. It is helpful, especially if you have a home office, to clear and clean the entire house, not just your working space, after a client leaves.

With all that said, even when I was single, I still had clients come to my home and never had a problem. You will want to have a way to screen clients before you invite them to your home. If you are intuitive, often you can tell on the phone if you like the person. I have my online scheduler set to confirm appointments so I have an opportunity to screen.

Also, I don't put my home address on marketing material or on my online scheduler so clients can't just show up at my home. A client has to schedule the appointment with me first, and then I send my home address. I am lucky to live with someone. Without wanting to sound sexist, if I am having a man over whom I have not met before, I have my husband here. If you don't have a mate, this person could be a friend who is visiting or a neighbor who has conveniently stopped by.

Screening is great, but sometimes the client brings a friend that is iffy. I usually have the person waiting sit in front of my big-screen TV, though one time I was a little concerned about the guest who was just a smidge too enthralled with my TV and might want to steal it! This is one reason why you might want to have a separate entrance to your office, or have your office away from the family area.

Yet I have never, ever had a problem with someone coming to my house who I thought was scary. But that is because I do screen. I've had people call me that made me uncomfortable, so I tell them I don't have a home appointment for two months and change them to a phone client until I can get a better feel of who they are.

LISA When working from home it is important to consider security. I'm lucky enough to have both a home office and a separate room where I meet with clients, which happens to be my meditation room. One of the concerns I had as a woman was having strangers, particularly men, come to my house when I was alone. I learned the hard way when I had a guy call me for a reading and the feeling he gave me over the phone was, well, creepy. Even though he didn't state anything that was obviously dangerous, I was having a bad intuitive feeling about him.

I became very uncomfortable anticipating meeting him and I ended up making other arrangements to meet him in a place where I was not alone. Interestingly, he ended up canceling his appointment. I realized that I was putting myself through unnecessary anxiety and discomfort so I changed my policies. Now for everyone I read for, I will only read in-person for people I have met before in a public event.

This is what my policy states: "NOTE! I only do private In-Person readings for those people I have met in person before! If we have not met in-person before, the best way to get an in-person reading with me is either when I am doing readings at a special public event or if we have met at a public workshop I have given. A PHONE READING is just as good as an in-person reading. See my FAQ for more detail."

Once I feel comfortable enough with someone to come to my home office, I will send him or her directions. I never post my home address on my emails and never on the Web. This is why it is good to have a PO Box as your work address in case you need to list a physical mailing address — it will keep your home address private.

You should also consider safety and security if you pick a business location that is not in your home. Working in a place that has other people present can be safer than if you are working alone somewhere at night.

Cindy makes a great point about the energy in your home. In our home we work very hard to keep the energy high and clean, particularly since my family is sensitive to the energy and we want to keep it at the level we prefer. My husband in particular doesn't want other people's negative energy floating around. Fortunately, through my intention and screening who comes to my house, we don't have any problems with energy left over by my clients. I also purposely have people come to my meditation and prayer room because the energy there is very high, maintained through my meditation and prayers.

Outside Office Location

SPIRITUAL BUSINESS TIP #8

Working with multiple practitioners is a wonderful way to network.

CINDY When starting a business that requires an outside office, but not a storefront for sales or walk-in traffic, it is often best to find a professional office, bookstore, or healing/New Age center that offers a per-diem room, which can be rented by the day or hour. These allow practitioners to rent an office without making a year-long lease commitment.

A friend of mine who owns a healing center requires a three-month commitment, yet the person needs only to take the room once a week. Sharing an office is another way to reduce the financial burden.

One marker to know if you are ready to start your business is having enough money put aside for one month's rent, one month's security, and the last month's rent. If you have that, you probably have thought out your business plan. If someone you want to share with doesn't have enough money put aside to pay half, that person probably will not be in the business for the long haul.

To avoid not starting at all because you would need too much money up front, it's better to need a bigger space or more days than not have enough business to support what you have. Also, you can always go bigger, it is harder to downsize if you have spent all your seed money up front.

LISA   The advantage of a public office space is that it gives you instant credibility and a professional image. If you are working as part of a group of practitioners, sometimes these public places will have a receptionist to schedule appointments, take messages, and collect payment. Some established groups of practitioners may even advertise for you. Also, having a receptionist helps with safety and security. All of this lends to your credibility and a professional appearance.

Shared Office

CINDY   Often a new practitioner will want to rent a work space, buy furniture, print a bazillion business cards and glossy brochures, and then sit and wait for customers to pile in. It is much more advantageous to first work with another practitioner or be part of a group.

It isn't the other person or group's responsibility to find your clients for you, but it is a way to network and share expenses so you don't have to look at your client as a dollar bill walking in the door.

I suggest you first look for a per-diem room or an office share. Often a healing practitioner or other spiritual entrepreneur doesn't work seven days a week. You might be able to help each other. Always make up a written agreement between parties to be clear about responsibilities on each side.. Understand that the following list isn't complete. Visit either of our websites for sample agreements.

Here are some things to consider when sharing a space:

- When will each of you use the room?
- Who is responsible to vacuum, take out the trash, etc?
- What scents can be used in the room?
- Where do things get stored?
- How is the room to be left?
- Who pays the landlord?
- When is the rent due?
- What happens if one of you is late with the rent?
- How much notice is required to end the partnership?
- Can you sublet?
- Who is responsible for finding a new practitioner if one of you leaves?

It is a sad but proven truth that just because you are a nice, spiritual being, it does not mean the other person, no matter how spiritual he or she may seem, has the same ethics or business sense. The nicest people have left the other person hanging because that nice person couldn't come up with the rent money and didn't 'fess up until the week before it was due.

If you are the one responsible for paying the rent, at the outset you should collect from the person you share with, the first and last month's rent, and even a month's security. It is important not to mix this money with your own funds. I recommend you open a free checking or savings account and put the security and last month's rent in it until it is needed. If the person doesn't have the money to pay two months' rent and security up front, he or she may not be a good partner to share space with.

Customer's Location

CINDY If I am going to the customer's location I make sure that I have everything I need to create a professional space for my session. I ask to have a private space, which is not always possible, at a psychic reading party where I am setting up my reading area at someone's home, office, or restaurant, but I do my best to make my space feel private. I ask that it be well lit with comfortable seating. Because I am sensitive to scents, I also ask that no scented candles or pot-pourri are near my space.

When I first started, I used to go to the customer's house for the reading. Now, I would not recommend doing that for many reasons. A few are safety, the wear and tear on your car, and it's hard to end the reading. When I was at someone's house, I felt as if I had to sit and chat after, which really prolonged the reading. If I am in my home, I can get up and walk the client to the door.

If you do choose to go to someone's home, you might consider charging for traveling time. A friend of mine suggests $5 per 20 miles. It isn't a lot, but enough to cover gas and wear on your car.

LISA When I did angel reading parties I had a few ground rules for the participants. One was that there was no alcohol allowed. I know that may rain on some people's parades, but alcohol and psychic readings do not mix, especially when you don't know who is going to be there. Many times the parties are a dual affair at which the hostess may add another form of entertainment such as selling jewelry or Tupperware and/or dinner.

If you are doing an angel party or a psychic reading party bring what you need to do readings with you — not just your divination tools, but also instructions on how the readings will be done and a sign-up sheet. I have a FAQ sheet that explains what my angel readings are like, what to expect during a reading, and how much the cost is and how to pay. I usually only take cash or a credit card, which you can easily do if you have a smartphone and use a PayPal or other merchant account app.

This way I know the payment has been made, rather than taking a check that may bounce. I also have a sign-up sheet for participants. There are no appointment times listed, but I know that I will do each reading for a limited time, such as 15 minutes each, and then leave myself 5 minutes between each reading for transition. This way I know how many readings I can do in a block of hours that I have available at the party.

Before the readings you may want to give a short talk to the group on what a reading is and how it will be done. Some readers like to do a demonstration reading to someone in the group first.

Over the Phone vs. In-Person

CINDY If you are a massage therapist or practice another service that needs the physical client in front of you, then you can skip this section. In my line of work, as a psychic, phone readings are great. Where else can you work in your pajamas? Although now with Skype and other video chats, pajamas are often out of the question! Working over the phone also allows me to travel. With today's technology, my clients don't even know I am out of town or even out of the country. Clients often find that phone sessions are more convenient and more relaxed.

The only time that's not true is when they have children to tend to or nosey mates. There are many positives, but phone sessions can have their pitfalls, including the lack of focus on the client's part and receiving timely payment. You need to have a good phone plan, good phone connection, good headset, and a good way to get paid.

Also, I find people forget phone reading appointments more than in-person sessions, but with today's online scheduling apps, which send emails to remind the client, that will most likely change.

LISA Most of my readings are done over the phone with clients all around the world. As Cindy says, working over the phone with clients is a great way to increase your freedom and work from anywhere, plus it makes it easier to schedule an appointment because neither of you have to travel. I find the phone tends to be more reliable than Skype because sometimes people don't have a good headset for their computer, which is necessary for clear sound and no feedback from speakers. Also, Skype can be flaky with the sound and cut out or make you sound like you're underwater.

If you use Skype, make sure you have a good headset and that you have a good Internet connection. Skype is a great alternative for international calling, though, because there is no cost involved. In setting up a phone appointment, I always tell people that a landline has the clearest sound, but today people often only have a cell phone as their main telephone.

For a cell phone connection, ask your clients to be in a place with a strong signal and where they won't be disturbed. Doing a reading or a phone consultation in the car when you're driving, for either of you, is a **bad** idea since you can't concentrate on your phone call or your driving. In the UK it is illegal, for good reasons, to use a cell phone while driving.

Keep in mind that not only should your client or customer be in a good cell signal location and a place where they won't be disturbed, you should be as well.

I also make the call to my client rather than have him or her call me; this is because I then control the timing. If you wait for clients to call you and they are late, your scheduling can be messed up. Set a policy that if you cannot reach them within 5–10 minutes they will need to reschedule with you.

As Cindy mentioned, phone appointments are more likely to be forgotten than in-person appointments. To reduce the number of no-shows for my appointments I use an online scheduler in which I enter in the appointments for both in-person and phone sessions and the scheduler will send them an email reminder the day before. This has reduced my no-shows to practically none.

There are online schedulers that you can use for free and then upgrade them to features such as taking payments or sending text message reminders. You may find it more difficult to end a session over the phone, but you can say a couple of minutes before the end of the session time, "We only have a couple of minutes more, so we'll have to start wrapping up."

Then at the end of the session you can say that you need to get on to your next appointment, whatever that may be, even if it is an appointment for you to work on your next project!

Clearing Your Workspace

CINDY Whether in an office or your home, it is important to clear your space of the client's energy after they leave. People leave energy behind, not only when they are releasing it but also when they are sitting waiting for their appointment. A wonderful way to clear a space comes from my book *Soul Soothers: Mini Meditations for Busy Lives*.

SPACE-CLEARING MEDITATION

1. Take three deep breaths, and with each exhalation, relax your shoulders.
2. Return to breathing normally.
3. Visualize the space you want to clear.
4. Imagine that the entire space is filled with a bright golden light as if there is a million-watt golden bulb in the center.
5. See the light reaching every corner and crevice.
6. Envision yourself now standing outside your space, seeing that beautiful, bright light coming out all the windows and doors.
7. Imagine that the intensity and brightness is growing.
8. Ask that only what is for the highest and most loving good for the occupants of the space be allowed to stay and all that is not be removed and sent to the light for healing.

LISA As Cindy mentions it is vitally important to clear and cleanse the energy of your working space not just for your next client but for you as well. If you are an energy healer, life coach, holistic healer, intuitive or psychic reader, or just work with people in general, which covers all businesses, managing the energy in your space is key to keeping the vibration free and clear of energy you do not want.

Raising the energy of your space also invites good positive energy in to help you and your business serve others. In my meditation space where I work with clients to do a reading or energy healing, many comment on how good it feels in the room as they enter.

There are many ways to clear the energy of a room and raise its energetic vibration so it has more positive divine energy within it. The important thing is to remember that your intention and thoughts are what energy follows. Like attracts like, so if your intention is to have a higher vibration of energy in your space that is full of love and positive, that will automatically bring in energy of that kind.

The rituals and prayers (which is an intention put into words) are a great way to immediately change the energy in a room. Following are more ways you can clear and raise the energy of your workspace.

Smudging

CINDY If you or your clients are not sensitive to smells and it is allowed by your landlord, another way to clear a workspace is through smudging. Make sure the smoke detector is temporarily deactivated, and don't use this method if you have a sprinkler system or you cannot temporarily deactivate the smoke detector. Better yet, avoid smoking the place up so much that it will set off the alarm. You do not need a ton of smoke; it is the intention that does the cleansing. Everyone smudges differently, but here is an easy way to do it.

1. Light a small piece of white sage or incense.
2. Open the windows and doors, if possible.
3. Walk around the room allowing the smoke to rise along the corners of the rooms, windows, and doors. Ask God/Spirit/Creator, etc., that anything not for the highest and most loving good for all those concerned be released through the smoke as it rises.
4. After you are done, imagine or see the room/house/office building surrounding in loving, protective golden or white light.
5. IMPORTANT: Reactivate the smoke detector.

Using Sound and Objects for Clearing

LISA Another way to clear the energy in your space is with sound. If you can do this without disturbing others who may be sharing your space or when no one else is around, it can be an easy and clean way to clear the energy. You can do this with music that you find uplifting and gives you a great positive feeling.

I often use recordings of chanting or kirtan, which is music that praises the Divine. Play your music for at least 5 to 10 minutes. If it is music you like and you enjoy either singing or dancing with it, do that because it intensifies the energy!

People often use Tingshas, which are small Tibetan cymbal bells, or Tibetan singing bowls — both ring a beautiful tone when struck. A tuning fork can work just as well; it is the sound vibration and the intention you put behind it that makes this work. You can walk in a circle slowly around the room while ringing the bells or bowls. Strike them gently so the sound reverberates in the room and strike it again only when the sound dies to silence.

Cindy mentioned that the items you have in your workspace hold energy, which can also change the energy in a room. I have a collection of crystals on several altars around the room that help hold a nice energetic vibration. With those items I also have icons, ie., statues and pictures, of things that have divine meaning to me. Because they invoke in me a particular feeling whenever I look at them, it raises and shifts the energy of my space.

HOW DO MY CLIENTS CONTACT ME?

LISA With technology moving at a fast pace, there are many options available for your customers to contact you. I always say, "If you can't reach me, you're not trying hard enough," because you can reach me through so many methods. Many of those methods are free or low-cost. Traditionally we think of contacting people through the phone or mail, now we can email, text, Skype, video-chat, and of course, make a phone call.

There are many different phone options you can choose from. Pick a few ways that people can reach you, such as a phone number and email address and put those on your contact listing. Many of these options are available for little or no cost.

CINDY My phone bill is the only thing in my business that keeps going down in cost. It used to cost me $350 a month for phone service — and that was just a landline. I now pay a small yearly fee for Skype that allows me unlimited calls to the United States and Canada, as well as have unlimited calling on my cell phone and landline.

Phone Number: Business vs. Home

CINDY   The phone is often the first "in-person" connection that you make with a new client. If your mate or your child picks up the phone with a simple hello, the client will most likely be confused, or worse, hang up thinking she has the wrong number. On top of that, it rings of unprofessionalism. It is better for the prospective client to get your professional message when she calls than the wrong person. We highly recommend a separate phone number, or as in my case, you being the only one who answers that phone.

My phone number is the same as my home number, but my husband doesn't answer my phone ... ever. We have no children, so that is not an issue. When I answer my phone I say, "*Cindy speaking,*" so it is clear that the prospective client dialed the correct number. My digital answering machine is set up with a business message, not a personal one. My friends and family know what I do and so this does not present a problem, except that my phone will sometimes ring in the middle of the night. I get more robot and fishing calls than if I did not use my home number for my business.

LISA   Cindy and I agree that a separate phone number for your business is extremely important. Not only does it give you a more professional image, and helps establish yours as a real business rather than a hobby run out of your home, it also can be a tax deduction as a business expense.

If you are working out of a home office, and you have a separate business line, you can turn off the business line phone or silence it when you do not want to be disturbed on your "off hours." You can also set up an answering machine message that is separate for your business.

I have always had a separate phone line for my business, and there are very inexpensive ways you can do this now with services such as Skype or add-on phone lines to an existing phone service. If a call comes in to my business line at night or on the weekend I know that it is a business call and not a personal call.

I take a slightly different approach to answering business calls in off hours; most of the time I don't do it. In fact, my business phone-answering message states, "If you are calling during non-business hours, I will return your call the next business day." The reason is I don't want clients to believe they have 24-hour access to me, but another reason is time management.

Managing your time is very important to any small business and so I focus my business time on business so I can have personal time for family and home life. If you have heavy family demands or children, you will need to manage your time so that your personal time is not eaten up by your business.

Managing your own business can be time-consuming, and being available for business calls 24/7 is a sure way to not have any time for anything else, which can be a disaster if you have other responsibilities or want to have a balanced life.

Another good reason to have a separate business phone number is that you can give it out to potential clients and not worry that you are giving out your private home number. There are many instances when you'll be asked for a business phone number. This usually happens when you are transacting business or filling out forms for your business.

You may also want to list your business number on your business cards, brochures, postcards or advertising in magazines or event programs. You may not want to publicly distribute your home phone number in all those places.

Even then be careful of putting your business phone number online, since spammers and telemarketers will easily get that number and call you. The worst thing is to put your phone number on your website. I made the mistake once of using my cell phone number as my business phone and put that number online.

Automated software programs, called "Crawlers," that search out information to copy and use without permission found my website business listing and my phone number and replicated the listing on directory sites that I had no control over.

Soon after that I began receiving so many telemarketing calls per hour I had to change the phone number! Can you imagine this happening to your home phone number? But there are ways around this by using a website contact form, which we'll talk about later in this chapter.

Other Phone Options: Cell Phones, Texting, Skype, Online Phone Numbers, and "Add a Line"

CINDY CELL PHONE: Having a cell phone is a great option. You can carry your office with you and not worry about missing or returning calls. I find my business flourishes when I answer a call when it comes in rather than returning the calls later. The downside is that you are always "on call," unless you choose to screen your calls. Screening calls is a fine option; so don't avoid a cell phone just because you don't want to be "always available."

Many people have a cell phone for their business and leave their home phone for the home. This is a good solution, yet still, you must always answer the cell phone professionally and remember to check messages frequently. The cell phone also allows people to text, which can be quite handy for setting up appointments, being notified if your client is running late, or even for quick follow-up questions. If you use your cell phone for business, I suggest a plan of unlimited calls and texting so you don't send out worry energy about cost instead of calm, healing energy, every time you get a text! Speaking of the phone bill, call up your phone carrier every six months to see if you can renegotiate your bill. You never know what specials are being run.

TEXT: Get an unlimited texting plan so you don't convey, "Oh no, please don't contact me" energy when clients text, because you are worrying about the charges. Clients will often text rather than call if they know you have a cell phone. Recently my clients have started to text me for appointments. I like the ease of answering in a text, but have found some problems, too.

I find clients think nothing of texting a quick question or asking for reassurance, which they wouldn't do if they had to call or email. So I have come up with a solution, the "quick question" rate. I charge a fee for quick questions that takes into account the time it takes to read the question, answer it, and type the answer. I make it very clear that the time it takes is probably longer than an actual appointment. I text my policy and ask clients if they really want me to take the time to answer a question, or would they rather set up an appointment. Sometimes they say yes, sometimes they choose to wait.

The important thing is that I don't get resentful toward texts. Personally I prefer texts to calls; it is fast, simple, and doesn't interrupt my day as much as a phone call. I just wish I could flag a text someway so I don't lose track of it. I am sure technology will allow that soon enough!

SKYPE and other online calling options: I have used Skype as a phone option for years now. You can Skype for free with anyone who has a Skype account or pay a small yearly fee to be able to Skype to any landline or cell phone. The only negative I have found is that you need a strong Internet connection or the call quality will sometime be lackluster.

A pro would be that you can also video chat, which many of my clients like because they can actually see me, but again, without a strong Internet connection, the quality can be iffy. When I was in the Dominican Republic, and the Internet was cooperating, I could call my US clients for free on Skype. I have clients from Africa, Australia, Portugal, Trinidad, and other countries that I speak with using Skype, as it is a common phone option for expats living overseas.

You can even download a separate program that allows you to record your session and then send the MP3 of the conversation on both Skype and iPhone. I once had a party of young girls whose mother couldn't afford to pay me to drive an hour and a half to come to her home, so we did a cheaper party with me on Skype. The girls loved it! To learn more about these Internet phone options, look up VoIP online.

FACETIME: On Apple devices, you can use the Facetime option, and the calls are free. You can see the person you are speaking with, and you can Facetime from your Apple computer or laptop, which is easier than trying to hold the phone up!

Apple does not have the corner on this market; there are many other online options for calling and video. Do some research and see what works best for you.

LISA GOOGLE HANGOUTS: Google now has their alternative to Facetime and Skype called Hangouts. Google Hangouts is integrated with Google Voice. You can make video calls, video conferencing as well as texting, and regular phone calling with Hangouts. Google Hangouts is becoming a powerful platform where you can also broadcast webinars straight to the Internet and then share a recording of it automatically on YouTube.

CINDY TOLL-FREE: I recently got rid of my toll-free number since most people have cell phones and long distance charges are a thing of the past. Most landline accounts also have unlimited local and long distance, so clients don't mind calling out of their area code, no longer put off by a long-distance phone number.

LISA "ADD A LINE:" Many phone services will allow you to add an additional line to your existing account for minimal cost. This is also the case for cell phone and cable company providers who offer a phone service. You often can get great rates for having more than one line on an account, and many offer great rates on international calling.

CINDY No matter what I choose, I have my phone numbers ring on my private phone number except my cell phone. My husband has his own phone so he doesn't answer my home phone. I have a remote phone number from when I had an office in Greenwich, CT and I have my private phone number. They all ring on one line. It is easy, except I would suggest setting it up so that you can tell which number a person is calling from. I have chosen not to have a separate business number, but if I were just starting out, I would have business and personal separate.

LISA A good thing about phone services these days are the features you can add on almost any phone. If you have several phone numbers you can use the "Find me" feature, which will allow a call to one phone number which will ring on other lines so you can pick up the call from those phones. You can also forward your phone to another phone number. I love the feature to have your voicemail message actually sent in an email along with a text message when the voicemail comes in.

I have an interesting story of how this technology allows you to be reached. After one of our vacation trips to Montreal we were driving home to southern New York. About 45 minutes into our 6-hour trip I received a text message that I had a voicemail message on my home phone from the police department. Needless to say I was a little shocked, but I was able to receive voicemail messages through email on my phone.

What had happened was the hotel we had just left thought the valet had left someone else's keys in our car and were desperately trying to find us. They didn't have our phone number but knew the town we lived in, so they called the police to see if they could get a message to us. The police called our private home phone number and left a message for the hotel. I was able to call the police back and find out what happened and then call the hotel to tell them we did not have the keys to the other car.

CINDY Lisa is right on about the convenience of receiving a phone message in your email or as a text. I travel extensively and like now, writing this from the Dominican Republic, if someone calls my home phone, I can get the message without having to call my phone line to retrieve it. I just click the email and the voice message comes through my computer. I have been able to return phone calls easily and the phone number the call came from is on my email so I don't have to struggle to find a pen!

LISA ONLINE PHONE NUMBERS: You can now get phone numbers online that forward to another phone number such as your home phone. Google and Yahoo offer this service for free. The service provides you with a "virtual" phone number that people can call or even text to.

Google Voice will also convert a voicemail message to text and then email you the message. I use Google Voice phone number on my website, which you can see on the contact page of my website. The useful thing about this service is that you can give out these phone numbers as your business phone number and eliminate the need to use your home phone.

Of course, if you call someone you will have to use a real phone, since you cannot make calls from these numbers only receive calls with them. Nevertheless, this gives you the benefit of having a separate business phone number and only pay for one phone line.

CINDY I wasn't aware of this option, but it makes great sense. You can save a lot of money by not having to get a separate phone line. I really like the idea of getting the message converted into text. Sometimes I am teaching a class or in a place where I don't want to be that obvious that I am taking a call. I can simply read the message and then decide how to respond.

Your Email Address

LISA Next to the phone, email is becoming the most common way people contact each other. It is almost universal these days that people ask for your email address before they ask for your phone number! Whether you use an email from your Internet Service Provider or a free email service such as Google or Yahoo, make sure to create an email address name that is easy for others to remember and easy for you to say.

Try not to use email address names with underscores or dashes in them because they're not easy to type. Often, people will use their first name, a dot or period and then their last name. If your last name is hard to spell, like mine, then use something that is easier to say and remember. If you can have an email address that uses your domain website name that is even better.

For example, my website is www.LMK88.com and my email address is AngelReadings@LMK88.com where my domain name is LMK88.com instead of gmail.com or yahoo.com. Using your hosted domain name gives you more of a professional image than using a free email address.

Just as with your business phone number, use a separate email address for your business. This will be the email address that you give out to everyone to contact you with regard to your business.

For those of you who are a little more technical, another way to "hide" your email address from "bots" but still list it online is to insert a graphic image or JPEG of your email address on your website. "Bots" cannot read the picture, but people can. A contact form allows people to contact you, eliminating the risk of telemarketers and spammers knowing your email address.

CINDY I like Lisa's idea of using your domain name in your email, yet avoid Info@domain name as the search engines sometimes see that as a typical spam address. I try to avoid using the letter L and O as well as the numbers 1 and Zero in email addresses.

In the case of Lisa or others whose name starts with L, they may want to use an L. So if you want to use L, capitalize it and same with the number 1, be sure to use a font that looks like the number 1 not the letter i or write it so that it clearly looks like a 1. I would avoid O and zero just because it is hard to tell the difference no matter what font you use.

Website Contact Forms

LISA Website contact forms are excellent ways to have people easily send you an email message without you giving out your email address. It's quick and easy for someone perusing your website, and if you ever change your email address, the person can still contact you. In fact, if you want to use your personal email address or a free email address a contact form still shows a professional image.

A website contact form looks like a form you'd see on paper, in which people enter information into boxes, click a button, and the form is sent automatically to you. On my website this is the only way you can contact me. If your website is built on Wordpress.com you can add a contact form to any page or post.

If you host your own Wordpress.org website there are plenty of plugins that are easy to use. My contact form automatically adds those who sent me a message to my email list with their permission. You can even have the contact form send the information to several email addresses, not just one.

The website contact form usually has text boxes to fill out for name, email address, subject, and message box. Most contact forms will then return a message to the sender saying that their message has been sent. This is a quick and easy way for people to contact you directly using email. I would suggest that you respond as quickly as possible so the sender doesn't think that the message went into a black hole.

Another nice tool you can use on your website as an alternative to placing your phone number online is to use a "click-to-call-me" button that will call you directly from a phone number that people enter into the form. These buttons are good because you don't display your business phone number or any phone number. The software will connect their phone number to yours, behind the scenes.

Other click-to-call-me buttons work for those who access your website with a mobile phone. Because they are already using their phone the button will call you from their phone directly. I use a free Skype "click-to-call-me" button that will pop up in their Skype application which then directly calls my Skype business phone number.

You can try the click-to-call-me button on my website on my "Contact" page. Leave me a message and let me know you're reading my book! If you ever decide to change your business phone number you don't need to worry that people won't be able to reach you because you can change the number behind the scenes and people can still use the button.

Online Booking Services

CINDY   I have just started using an online booking service and I am surprised how well it is working out. It is a bit time-consuming to set up, but once you have it running, your clients can go online to book appointments. I have it set up so that I confirm the client's time before the appointment is set. The client must book his or her appointment 48 hours in advance, so that I can plan my day without worrying about a last-minute appointment being added.

Not everyone likes to go online, so if a client doesn't like the online service or wants to see if she can get in sooner, she can still call, email, message or text me.

I am eager to see how this online service works out. The one I am using currently is free unless I want to add PayPal so my clients can pay in advance. If enough of my clients use it, I will consider going to the paid level. It works well for a location with multiple practitioners because whoever answers the phone can book an appointment for anyone in the office and know they are not double booking or booking when the practitioner doesn't want to work.

LISA   I've been using an online booking system for many years now, mostly for the appointment reminder feature. I found that – especially for phone sessions – people will forget they have an appointment. I used to email people a reminder, and then, being the technical person I am, I knew there had to be a better way.

Now there are a number of choices for online appointment schedulers and reminder programs. An online scheduler can also automatically put an entry into my calendar for that appointment. I am the only one who enters in appointments, and the system will send my client and me a reminder the day before.

I also have the system set up to ask for payment as well if my client has not paid me at the time of setting up the appointment. It is all automated so it saves me extra work.

CINDY   Now that you know where you are going to set up shop, how your clients will contact you, and have started to experiment with some marketing material, we will talk in Chapter 4 about the startup costs you will encounter and getting paid for your services.

CHAPTER FOUR

Money and Spirituality

• • • • • • • • • • • • • • •

MONEY IS NOT EVIL!

SPIRITUAL BUSINESS TIP #9

Money is not evil. Money is good.

CINDY Money is not evil. Money is good; it represents an exchange of energy. Because we have money, we can continue to be of service. It is necessary so that you can pay your rent, your telephone, and your car payment. I have a saying, *"You pay your plumber, you pay your psychic. We both need to make a living."* Both the psychic and the plumber offer a service. There is nothing inherently wrong with making money.

It is how you feel about money, just as it is your attitude toward your business that will decide if it is spiritual or not. For many reasons, money has gotten a bad rap in the spiritual community. The issue around money and spirituality may relate to the collective unconscious or go back to past life memories of being a monk who disavowed bodily comforts.

Even Buddha saw that this lack of attention to life's basic needs was not the way to enlightenment. He taught the importance of taking care of your body and your needs in order to be able to flourish on your spiritual path.

At first, the money you make from your spiritual practice should pay for marketing and improvements to your business, rather than supporting you. After all, a new mainstream business would not expect to make a profit for up to a year or more and it is no different in a spiritual business. To have a successful long-lasting venture, you want to give your business the strongest financial foundation that you can.

My best advice about money and starting a spiritual business is to keep your day job. One of the biggest mistakes you can make is to quit your day job before your business can support itself. If you struggle to pay bills, you may find that your energy is filled with financial worries. If you have to look at a client as a dollar sign, it is almost guaranteed that clients either won't come or won't come back a second time.

Slowing the growth of your business expenses as your business grows can help guarantee a stronger business in the long run. Start small to avoid financial problems, and realize it is your job to support the business's growth before you expect it to support you. You may not have everything you want for your business in the beginning, and that is to be expected. You don't need the fancy brochure or the top-of-the-line massage table right away. Although you might want to wait to open your business if you cannot afford some staples. These are covered later in this chapter.

SPIRITUAL BUSINESS TIP #10

There is nothing *unspiritual* about wanting enough income to pay your bills.

LISA As Cindy pointed out, money is just another form of energy circulating through giving and receiving. If you want to give you have to receive. It's a law of nature and the Universe that there must be a balance. If you are only giving then something will suffer until the balance returns. That suffering is usually because when you give without receiving you end up depleting yourself both energetically and materially.

Allow yourself to replenish yourself energetically and materially. Plus, the more you receive the more you can give. If you want to help more people you'll have to receive more money. It's as simple as that!

People have different views and attitudes about money, what is a lot of money to me may not be a lot of money to you. Your attitude toward money can change, as mine did. When I was growing up my family was pretty solidly middle class. There was not a lot of extra money floating around, and my parents were very frugal. Perhaps it was because we are Chinese and come from a culture of working hard but saving and carefully budgeting out what money you had. Growing up this way, I learned to spend wisely.

I remember in school being given only one BIC pen and no spares, even though BIC pens were inexpensive and almost disposable. Because of this I would make sure I didn't lose my pen and used it until there was no ink left. Only then was I allowed to get another one.

As time went by, and I became a working adult making my own money, I carried my frugality with me, watching prices in every item I picked in the store. In some ways, I was a little extreme. After I was married, my husband said I shouldn't worry so much, we have a good income and we expected it to grow as time went by.

Our incomes did grow and I tried to let go of some of my old habits of frugality, which kept me in the frame of mind of "lack." I changed my old attitude toward money to having "more than enough." This is not to say that I was careless with my money; I was still conscious of what I spent but had a different attitude.

This shifted the energy and the flow to more abundance. The important thing is that we didn't just sit back and expect the money flow to increase: it was coupled with a lot of hard work. Working hard toward your goals, shifting your attitude toward money to believing, "I can make more and will make more," allows you to be freer to move in that direction.

Your attitude toward money may also be one of "lack." Many times, as they say, you have to spend money to make money, particularly in the beginning. But spend wisely and work hard to learn what kind of investments to make in your business. Marketing is one of the best investments you can make because it will bring more customers in.

People always want more in life and they then seek out spiritual or metaphysical ways to bring in abundance in the form of material things and money. But the Universe cannot bring you that abundance without your getting involved. When I decided to really focus and work hard on making my business grow, I asked the Universe to bring me more customers. The answer I received was: create more products and services that people can buy and focus on marketing. I realized that both of those required work and education. Learning more about how to grow your business; in this case for me it was learning specifically how to market my kind of spiritual business, which should be and will be an ongoing process for you that should never end.

Business development requires constant education, and you are doing just that by reading this book! Learning how to market your business is hard work. To begin the work process you need to set your intention on a goal to build a business that will generate income.

Setting Your Intention

SPIRITUAL BUSINESS TIP #11

Your actions provide the Universe with the energy needed to bring about abundance.

CINDY Setting your intention for abundance is good, yet intention alone won't pay the bills. Fear cancels intention every time. I still set my intention to attract abundance, yet I make sure that I am being practical and realistic. Intention needs to be followed up with action and more follow-up. In my life, if I need a new computer or some other expensive item, this is what I do:

1. Figure out how much I need.
2. Put that amount "out to the Universe."
3. Follow up with action, usually in the form of extra marketing or quicker response time to client calls, so that the Universe has energy to work with.
4. Trust that the money will show up, but don't buy the item until it does.

I won't buy a computer on a credit card unless the old one has totally died and I have no other choice. With that said, if I feel my computer is on its way out, I start the intention and action right then instead of waiting for the crisis. Plus it doesn't hurt to have an "Oh no!" fund. We cover this later in the chapter.

I have found that the Universe will give hints of an impending financial expense and, if I don't bury my head in the sand, I'll have enough time to earn the money to take care of it.

After I set my intention for how much money I need, my agreement with Spirit is that I will answer the phone instead of letting the answer machine get it. I have limits: I only answer the phone between 10 a.m. and 9 p.m. It is amazing, but when I answer instead of letting the machine pick up, the calls start to come in more frequently and the money starts to accumulate. I am adding my energy to my intention of earning a strong income. I also need to step up my marketing and social networking to further support the Universe's efforts.

If you want the Universe to support your intention, you need to provide the energy to make it happen. This energy may be an action like my answering the phone or you may need to send out an email. You'll find that you need to spend a little to make a little. That spending might be in time or energy if not in cash. Some suggestions of ways to provide the energy in a form other than cash:

1. Go to events that you would normally skip so that your energy is present in the community.
2. Create and send an email with a "this month only" special.

3. Clean your office space and rearrange things to freshen up the energy.
4. Start a morning ritual of gratitude for what you have already.
5. Perform some community service or donate clothes and other items.

There is nothing *unspiritual* about wanting enough income to pay your bills and having a nice life, and there is nothing wrong for asking Spirit to help. Even Saint Francis de Sales knew that you need to take care of temporal (daily) affairs, and he also asked for help from above:

> *Make friends with the angels,*
> *who though invisible are always with you.*
> *Often invoke them, constantly praise them,*
> *and make good use of their help and assistance in*
> *all your temporal and spiritual affairs.*

Another important lesson I have learned over 20-plus years of business is to not hoard cash. If you are starting your business, you will most likely have a lot more expenses than you have income, so hiding cash from the government is a waste of time. It also sends the Universe the message, "*I am afraid I won't have enough.*" Everything I make gets deposited and all gets officially counted.

Giving Back

CINDY   When you love what you do for a living, even if it is your second job, you don't need as many toys, shoes, or other shopping distractions. You can accumulate less and give more. One way to assure financial abundance is to show your gratitude by giving back to your community in some way. You can offer a free class or promotion, which doubles as a marketing strategy. You can volunteer for an organization that you believe in.

For 13 years, I gave a free lecture at Borders Bookstore, might it rest in peace, called "Metaphysics Interactive." It was one of the best experiences I ever had. I intended it to be a marketing technique in the beginning. I had just moved to the Syracuse area, and a free lecture series was a way to get my name out. After a year or two, Metaphysics Interactive was my favorite night of the month and my way to give back to my community.

WHAT DO I CHARGE?

What Is the Going Rate?

SPIRITUAL BUSINESS TIP #12

When you first start, price yourself in the middle of what others charge in your area.

CINDY   A good rule to follow when you are first starting out is to price yourself in the middle of what others in your local area charge. You never want to be the most expensive or the cheapest. Cheapest means "not as good" in people's eyes, yet highest price is not seen as highest quality.

Check out what others are charging in the area. As mentioned earlier, experience what other practitioners in your field are offering and pay the full price. Take time after your session to think about how you value the work you just received. You will soon be able to see how you compare to others in your field and you will be able to price appropriately. It bears repeating: avoid being the most or least expensive.

LISA   Cindy makes a good point regarding going out to see what others in your line of business are charging. In this way you are doing your own market research to see what people in your location will pay. If you have a business that brings in clients from farther away, or even internationally, you can still set your price based on what the going rate is for what you do.

I draw clients from around the world, but have my prices based in US dollars. I don't change the rate for those in other countries. My personal preference is to do my in-person sessions in increments of 30 minutes because it is easier to manage calculating my rates in multiples of half an hour.

These rates are the same for my time to work with someone in-person, whether getting an angel reading from me, having a private guided meditation session with me, or my teaching them intuition lessons privately. It is just simpler for me to offer a price for my time this way. I used to offer lower priced services but now it's simpler and clients seem to be okay with it.

In the past I'd found with angel readings that a 15-minute session often ended up being at least 30 minutes because my customer would often want to go longer, so eventually it didn't make sense to offer less than 30 minutes. Other people who do readings, including Cindy, will do smaller increments with a variation on price to give incentives to purchase longer sessions.

Providing incentives to do longer sessions from shorter ones is a great way to have different service level offerings to accommodate different needs, particularly with readings.

CINDY Yes, as Lisa mentions, different providers will find their clients have different needs. I find the majority of my clients take the half-hour to an hour session and use the shorter sessions if they just have a quick question or want to follow up on an issue they are working on. The shorter session is also helpful for my first-time clients to get to know me with less risk.

Free vs. Charge

CINDY Offering your service free is a charity, not a business, and charities are run differently. If you want to start a charity, that's fine. Even if you decide not to charge for your sessions, you can still use the tips on marketing and some other parts of *Grow Your Spiritual Business* to help you grow your community service organization or charity.

LISA When I was advertising in a give-away magazine, I received a lot of inquiries for free readings. That shouldn't have surprised me but I had to come up with what to tell people. Without money you can't have a business, without a business you can't be of service, without being of service you don't have a spiritual business. Even "non-profit" make money to sustain their enterprise. The way I offer "free" readings is on my radio show. We often open up the lines for listeners to call in for a quick one-question reading. I tell people that if they want a free reading they can call in to the radio show.

CINDY That is a wonderful reminder that it is important to find a way to give back to your clients, be it through writing articles, being available on a radio show, giving a free talk, or maybe through a contest in which the prize is a free product. By giving back in some way, it is a win-win situation! Clients get something of value from you for free and you have a way to be of service and give people a chance to see your product or talent.

Value and Self-Worth
Self-Worth

CINDY When a practitioner has trouble charging for services, it often comes down to appreciating the value of what he or she does. If you are struggling with this, consider what you as an individual can offer that others in your field do not. Maybe you have a more compassionate attitude or are a better than average listener. Maybe you have learned a technique and added your own touch to it.

What benefit can you bring the client over and above what your chosen technique offers? Ask others who have experienced your service to write a testimonial so that you can see how they value your work. If you still have trouble charging for your services, you may want to do some soul search-ing to see what is blocking you from being able to recognize and assert your true value.

Your Value

SPIRITUAL BUSINESS TIP #13

The best way to know the value of your service is to experience similar practitioners.

CINDY What is your value, what do you add to your profession? If you are reading this book from cover to cover, you have already learned that the best way to know your value is to experience other practitioners or businesses that are similar to what you are offering. Remember how, back in Chapter 2 you looked at what you offer that others don't and how your work transforms your clients. Also, remember that Lisa suggested you look at the feedback from others. Both these techniques will help you to understand your value.

Once you have decided what your fee should be, if you still have trouble with charging what you feel you are worth, have someone else book your appointments for you. Give the scheduler your fees and don't give him or her permission to adjust the fee. If a client wants to negotiate your fee, have the appointment taker ask him or her to call you directly, at a time that is convenient for you.

If the client is willing to go through the extra effort, at your convenience rather than his or hers, then you may feel that you can make a one time discount or some other arrangement for payment compensation.

I recommend you stay away from bartering and sliding scale prices. Sliding scale can create an unhealthy situation in which your client may subconsciously feel she is not able to improve on her life because she would need to pay more or that she is not as worthy or getting the same treatment as a full-paying client. Avoid barter because it is very hard to have an equal barter. Either both sides feel they got the bad end or one feels guilty. It usually works better to pay the person for his or her service and then the person can pay you for your service.

LISA I agree with Cindy on price. Stick to your prices, and often you'll find you can be paid more than you think. Resist the urge to lower your price to get more business. Remember, once you lower your price it will be hard to raise it later. It would be better to offer a special discount that has an expiration date so you can return to your regular prices later. This gives customers an incentive to try out your business.

Avoid Victim Consciousness

CINDY Avoid falling prey to other people's victim consciousness; this is easier said than done. People who claim they can't afford to pay will often then go out and spend money on something else. I view my business, psychic readings, as a luxury and not a necessity. Your business may be different. When people can't afford my rates, which I feel are reasonable, I don't feel as if I'm depriving them. I simply suggest they call me back when they can afford the shortest session I have, which at this point is about the cost of a dinner for two at a local restaurant.

Some practitioners choose to charge based on a sliding scale, yet this often "enables" the client, keeping him or her from getting her life together because then she would have to pay full price. Better to have someone save up or wait until he can afford a session (or whatever you are offering) than to risk being an enabler.

There are many books written on co-dependency and the issues of enabling versus empowering others. If you are helping your client to not need you anymore, you are empowering them. The best sign you are doing it right is when you get referrals from clients who have been able to move forward and live their lives in an independent, healthy manner and respect your process enough to recommend others.

LISA Often people can pay, as Cindy mentioned. Many people like to bargain or see if they can get a price break. It is simpler not to have a lot of different pricing structures.

A compromise approach is to price small increments against longer sessions where you could charge $35 for a 15-minute session, but for a 30-minutes session you would charge $60. This gives people an incentive to purchase the longer session for a price break.

You Get What You Pay For

CINDY "You get what you pay for" is not just a saying. People truly believe it. The quickest way to have a client not take you seriously is to offer your service cheap, or worse, for free. So, once you are ready to call your business a business and not a hobby or charity, I recommend no barters or freebies. You can still run a contest for a free session or give a gift certificate for a discounted session to a valued client.

I sometimes send a discount coupon to my clients on birthdays or a holiday. Charging for your service is how you show yourself and everyone else that your time and your talent are valuable. Freebies are for when you are just learning, before you open your business doors, or, as you will learn in Chapter 5, to attract new clients.

Once your service becomes a spiritual business, it is a business. There are always exceptions. I never charge one particular friend, but I say it is a birthday present or holiday present. She doesn't take advantage of it, and if she did, I would start to charge her.

LISA "Market value" is defined as what the market, ie., your customers, will pay for your services. My rates are higher than many practitioners', for a couple of reasons. First, I believe I am worth it and so do my customers; they are willing to pay my rate. Second, my rate keeps out the people who are not really serious about getting a reading. This means, only the people who really desire having a reading with me and are willing to make the investment in the kind of readings I offer will pay my rate.

I used to offer lower-priced services but now it's simpler to only offer a 30-minute and 60-minute session, and clients are okay with it. It works better for my clients, rather than doing a 15-minute reading then add another 15 minutes when the first 15 minutes are up. Usually I have found that the shorter sessions are not enough for most people, and during the session even they don't want to keep within the short time frame. Often people will start with 30-minute sessions and end up adding another to do an hour.

Charging Friends

CINDY When you are first practicing and still not charging for your services, you might say something like, "*Once I open my office (go professional, etc.), this service would cost you X amount.*" When family or friends ask how much they owe me — although you could say the same even if they don't offer to pay you — I often say, "*Oh, the first one is free, but if you*

found it helpful and want another session, then I'll charge you x-amount."
Then it is important that you stick to it. You can always give a gift of your service as a birthday or holiday present or hand out discount coupons as part of a "New Business" special, yet make sure these have expiration dates on them!

LISA Most of the time friends expect to pay, but I don't charge them, and they don't abuse it. I usually don't charge my family, and most of them don't push for a free reading. They often ask to pay and I don't take it.

HOW DO I GET PAID?

CINDY Once you know what you are going to charge, you need to figure out how you are going to get paid. There are so many different options available now and with credit cards and debit cards being so prevalent, it makes sense to be a credit-friendly business.

Cash, Check or Charge?

LISA Long ago, cashiers were trained to ask a customer, "Cash, check or charge?" when someone walked up to the register. Those were the forms of payment available, and they pretty much still are. Cash is always a good form of payment. People often prefer to pay with a check rather than cash or a credit card. Personal checks can have the risk of not clearing due to insufficient funds in someone's account.

Over the years I have not received one bad check, so for my client base the risk may be low. The bonus in taking credit cards is that the credit card company guarantees payment once the transaction is approved and the money is deposited directly into your bank account. Many customers prefer to pay with a credit card and for some that's the only way they can pay.

The downside to taking credit cards is the small fee on each transaction, paid to the credit card company. The fee is often worth the ease and guarantee of payment you get in exchange. Refunds through credit cards are easy, though be aware you will be charged a transaction fee at both ends; when the card was charged and when the refund is made.

CINDY I know a number of psychics and other spiritual practitioners who still don't take credit cards. There is nothing saying you have to take credit cards or PayPal, but okay, I'm going to say it: accepting credit cards or PayPal is a must.

Many people don't carry around cash and simply expect you will accept credit cards. Plus, when offering services or sales over the phone, accepting credit cards avoids the person needing to mail a check. I have never met anyone who after deciding to take the leap to accepting credit cards or PayPal said it was a bad move.

However I have had practitioners, myself included, regret being roped into a traditional bank credit card system as the fees and percentage of each payment that they take has gotten quite high over the years. Traditional credit card systems also usually require contracts and they are very difficult and costly to break.

Online and Mobile Credit Card Processing

CINDY There are many different credit card options available to today's spiritual businesses. When I first started there were only the traditional bank options for accepting credit cards, with monthly fees and sales fees on top of the percentage of the sale. I actually had to pretend that I was a storefront business that sold metaphysical items instead of a psychic because I started at the height of the "1-800 phone psychic fiasco."

The banks didn't want to deal with all the charge backs, which were when a client said she did not purchase anything from the psychic and the credit card company had to return her money. I was told to fib by the credit card representative, and I was very uncomfortable about that. In over 20 years, I have only had one person try to deny the charges, but the 1-800 psychic businesses gave all of us a bad credit report as far as banks were concerned.

These days, you don't even have to be a business to accept credit cards; college kids can do it when they split up the cost of pizza! It is all managed online and all you need is a smartphone, computer or tablet connected to the Internet, or you can use your cell phone data service.

Make sure to compare rates and services charges. I get charged slightly more if I hand-enter the card number, but because I do a lot of work over the phone, this option is a must for me.

LISA The Internet has transformed the way we do business, particularly in handling financial transactions. Soon, using "eWallets" you'll be able to collect payment by someone sending you money using their smartphone. Currently, what is most accessible to the small business owner is taking credit card payments online and over the Internet.

As Cindy mentioned you can use PayPal, which is probably the easiest; with it you take credit card payments online with a personal PayPal account or with a business account. The downside to PayPal is that the money is deposited into your PayPal account, not your bank account. You must transfer the money to your bank account manually; it is not automatic.

In other online credit card processing systems your money is deposited directly to your bank account. Square, Stripe, Intuit and Flint are services that small businesses currently use. These are excellent services because they often do not cost anything to set up and the only fees you pay are transaction fees.

If you have a smartphone, laptop or tablet they also provide, free, a small plastic device called a dongle, which you use to swipe a credit card. Don't worry if you don't have the client's credit card in your hand to swipe. You can accept credit cards over the phone by typing in the client's credit card information on the app or website.

The service that I use from Intuit merchant services even allows you to take a photograph of the credit card and it will recognize the numbers. These systems also take debit cards. There is no reason nowadays to avoid taking credit cards as payment. I also find credit cards make it much easier for people to pay me for high-priced items such as my in-person weekend classes.

WHAT IS MY INVESTMENT?

CINDY It is important to start your business on a firm financial footing. If you have not saved up enough to start your business properly, it will be more difficult to make a strong profit. A start-up business needs a budget for launching, and there are things you should have funds on hand for before you make up your business cards. These may seem like no-brainers, but I have seen many spiritual businesses fail because they did not have certain start-up expenses covered. With that said, it is critical to be able to support yourself before you can expect to support the needs of your business.

Separate Business Bank Account

CINDY Maintaining a separate bank account is not as costly as it used to be. Many banks offer free accounts for business. They do bundles that include a free savings account. More for tax reasons than anything else, a separate bank account makes sense. You can get a debit card for your account and then it is very easy to keep all your business purchases separate from your personal.

So at tax time, you simply go to your accounting software, which has been downloading your business banking all year long, and pull a report for your accountant with all your income and expenses.

P.O. Box or Other Mail Service

CINDY Unless you have an office with mail delivery, I recommend a post office or some other outside mail delivery place. I use United Parcel Service's UPS Store as my post office because I can have packages delivered, and if I am on the road for a book tour, I know my items are not out on my front porch getting rained on. The cost of a P.O. Box or other service is quite low. I also like an outside mail service because I don't put my home address on my website, business cards, and promotional material. I don't want a client coming to my home at 10 o'clock at night looking for a reading!

LISA I also switched over to using the UPS Store mailboxes from the United States Postal Service P.O. boxes because I found that there were a lot more advantages. Because the UPS Store mailbox is considered a physical location you can ship many things to it that you cannot ship to a P.O. Box. There is always someone there to sign for a package so you don't need to worry about being available when the package is delivered.

Also, they notify you when you get mail or a package, and keep a record of when a package was delivered to you. In some locations you have 24-hour access to your mailbox. You do not have these services with a P.O. Box.

The other thing I have noticed is that you don't get as much junk mail. An actual physical location for your mailbox gives your business a little more credibility than an address that includes P.O. Box. As Cindy says, you also don't need to give out your home address whenever a work address is requested.

Computer

CINDY A reliable and relatively new computer is a necessity for any small business. Most of your more cost-effective marketing will be done online. You may not need a $3,000 Apple MacBook Pro, but you must have a computer with the ability to access the Internet with good speed and have enough memory to handle uploading and downloading large files as well as accounting, emailing and database programs, and decent-quality photo-editing software.

As your business grows, the ability to do webcasting and VoIP (Voice over Internet Protocol) may become important as well.

If you are not computer savvy, I highly recommend attending some computer classes at your local adult education center. To have someone else do your computer work when you are first starting out may seem like a great timesaver, yet every time you need to make a change you will have to contact and pay your computer guy or gal. This can be clumsy and costly, especially if you want to post to Facebook or keep your website current with specials and tips.

Adequate Internet

CINDY The Internet is your connection to your marketing and to your clients. You'll need to be able to respond to emails, messages, and data contact forms quickly. In order to keep your websites, social media, and other online contact frequent and up to date, you also need to have good Internet service and reliability.

You do not need the fastest or most expensive level of service, yet the slower the Internet speed, the longer it will take you each time you're responding to clients or marketing your business. Time is money — plus I value my sanity. When we travel out of the country and are stuck with lousy Internet, we have to put a lot of our business on hold. We can only write and respond to business early in the morning or late at night when our Internet allows. I am not able to Skype with my clients back home unless I purchase faster Internet access from the hotel or wherever, and that doesn't always work out. I have lost a lot of money simply because of a slow and unreliable Internet.

Telephones

CINDY As discussed in Chapter 3, there are multiple telephone options. You can have a traditional landline, a cell phone, an Internet phone number, or VoIP like Skype. You can get online phone numbers for free. Lisa gave some good options for you as far as these online types of phone services and a way to even get a free phone number.

Audio Recording Devices

CINDY Not every type of spiritual business needs to record encounters with clients, yet for those who do any type of Spiritual Counseling, Coaching, Angel Readings, Psychic Readings, or any work in which you talk to your client, a recording of the session is a plus and can set you ahead of others in your profession who do not record.

The two most up-to-date ways to record a session is on either a CD or an MP3 recording. Even a CD recording is becoming outdated. It is hard to keep up with the technology yet that is no excuse not to be as up to date as possible. You can go online for CD recorders. They are not cheap. My last CD recorder, a Roland CD-2i, cost me $700! For under $5, I purchased an add-on for Skype that allows me to record and create an MP3 of a client's session.

You can also get an MP3 recorder and email the MP3 file or download it to a CD. I recently purchased a $10 app for recording my cell phone calls. I really like this new option and am converting to using my cell phone for client calls instead of my landline.

LISA I used to offer recordings for clients who wanted to record their sessions. For the phone I had an elaborate setup that would record to my computer and for in-person sessions I used a cassette recorder. But technology has changed all that so quickly! I no longer offer recordings, partly because it was a hassle to get the recording transferred to a CD and ship it to the client, but also because many people can record on their smartphone or other device.

There is usually an app that can be downloaded for recording, or the phone comes with a way to record sound. The sound recording quality on smartphones is pretty amazing these days.

Insurance Agent & Lawyer

LISA Do you need to hire a lawyer or insurance agent? Only when you need them, and you won't need them all the time.

Insurance is always a smart thing to have, both for your workplace and for you. Liability insurance is important to protect you from any accidents that may happen to your customers. If you have insurance already your homeowner's policy may have an umbrella clause that will cover other things.

Unfortunately there is no insurance for psychic readings, but you can get liability insurance for energy healing work such as Reiki, EFT or QiGong, etc.

If you are teaching classes, holding retreats, seminars or workshops you can get event insurance. If you search online for event insurance or energy healing practitioner insurance you can find out more information about how to get these types of insurances. Many rental locations for events require that you have liability insurance.

CINDY I carry an umbrella policy that protects me from some incidents like a client falling on my steps, yet you might want business insurance or add a rider based on your specific needs. The best thing is to have an honest conversation with your insurance agent about what you do and where you do it, as insurance coverage varies from state to state.

LISA Of course, you don't want to wait until you really need a lawyer, so have a lawyer in your contacts list. Lawyers are good for helping with legal questions about your business.

For example, say you want to rent a place for your business; the lease agreement may be a bit more complicated than a normal apartment rental agreement. You may also have to draw up a contract for doing business with another business or with an individual. You can have a lawyer look the contract over for you and help advocate for your side in negotiating terms in the agreement that are fair and favorable to you. A lawyer can check to make sure there aren't any terms that may create a problem for you.

Also, you may want to protect yourself from liability in your business. To do that you may want to set up a legal entity for your business, of which there are many to choose from. For example, you can set up your business as a Limited Liability Company (LLC), an S-Corporation, or other legal entity.

Don't be intimidated by the terms, it's really not that bad. The advantage of setting up a legal business entity is that your liability is limited, so your personal assets are not at risk. My business is set up as an S-Corporation, for a small business which means that my company gets paid, and payments are then passed through to me personally.

I don't need to use my Social Security number because I use the company's EIN number. A lawyer and accountant can help you decide which is best for you since each structure has advantages legally and tax-wise. Here in the United States, every state has its own laws regarding business and lawyers can help you with that as well.

Incorporating vs. Sole Proprietor

LISA The main consideration when choosing between incorporating your business and running your business without incorporation is liability protection. If you do not incorporate your business you can still own your own business as an individual. This is called a Sole Proprietorship. The business and you personally are seen as one entity and you, as the owner, are personally responsible for any liabilities of the business.

If your business is sued for breaking a legal contract, for example, not paying rent for your place of business, or for injury incurred or uncollected debts, and so on, you are personally liable. The court can go after your personal assets if you are seen as at fault.

If you do incorporate your business, and there are many kinds of incorporations you can do, then the liability is the responsibility of the business. This protects your personal assets from any suits against the business, except in extraordinary circumstances.

Cindy and I are not lawyers and we cannot give you any legal advice, so consult a lawyer to get the proper information about what is best for you.

You may have heard the term "DBA," which means "Doing Business As." In other countries they may use the term "TA" or "Trading As." These are not business structures per se, but a legal term meaning that you are conducting business under another name or "fictitious name."

To set up a DBA you need to legally file it as your business name, which a lawyer can do for you. You can have a DBA as a Sole Proprietor or as an incorporated business. Having a DBA does not necessarily mean that the business is incorporated.

My legal incorporated business is called "LMK88 Inc.," but my DBA is "Lisa K." Having a DBA makes it much easier for my customers and me. When clients make out checks to pay my business or me it is one name, "Lisa K." This also maintains my branding and is why this book is co-authored by "Lisa K.," which keeps my brand identity consistent.

Accountant

CINDY An accountant is a no-brainer need for your business. You have many choices of how to keep your financial records, but no matter which you choose, doing your taxes on your own for a small business can result in lost deductions — or worse, claiming the wrong deductions. Your accountant can also help you set up bookkeeping software or at least teach you how to organize your receipts for tax time.

Being a service provider or selling a product creates a big difference in how you pay your taxes. Sales tax can be tricky and may require payment more than once a year. A good accountant can help you with all the ins and outs of the financial end of your business. Taxes vary by state and even by city so don't assume your brother-in-law who owns his own accounting business and who lives in another area can properly advise you on your bookkeeping and taxes.

LISA   Of all expenses, an accountant is a must, particularly because taxes for a business are a bit more complex than your personal taxes. You'll want to take advantage of any tax breaks that are available for your business. An accountant can help you with business tax deductions. Accountants can tell you what expenses you can deduct and which ones you can't.

They can also tell you how to keep your business expenses separate from your personal ones so you can claim deductions. For example, if you use a room in your home, or a computer for work, you can deduct some of the expenses for these under certain conditions. There are also advantages tax-wise to being incorporated.

Cindy and I are not accountants so we cannot give you any accounting advice, but a good Certified Public Accountant (CPA) is not hard to find and he or she can give you advice for your particular business setup. Having a CPA do your taxes is well worth the cost.

Accounting Software

CINDY   I use accounting software that connects with my bank so that I can download activity from the bank. This way, I can put each transaction into the proper category. I do this every day or every other day so I don't forget what the purchase was for, and it only takes me a few minutes at most. I also try to use my debit card for everything business so that (1) I have a record besides the receipt; and (2) if the business can't afford it, I won't buy it.

My accounting software, Quicken for Mac, also allows a cash account in which I track all my cash purchases. At the end of the year, I can simply pull up a report and take that to my accountant.

Phone apps are available for tracking business expenses when on a trip. You can take pictures of your receipts and then download all the information into a spreadsheet. With technology, you can track your income and expenses so accurately that there is no excuse for not having a grasp on the profitability of your business at any given time or for dealing with the "shoe box full of receipts" nightmare at tax time.

LISA Accounting programs both online and for your computer make it very easy to manage finances for your business. I use Quickbooks for my business and Quicken for my personal finances. Both of these are made by Intuit and have been around for over 20 years. My first Quicken entry was in 1994! There are many more options these days, though these seem to be the most popular.

You can link your bank account to these programs and download your bank transactions to Quicken or Quickbooks. I also download my credit card transactions to these programs to keep track of what I spend. You can categorize the kind of income and expense you enter for each transaction and then create reports on what you earned and spent for the year.

For example, you can have a category for marketing and include payments for print advertising and/or online advertising. The report then will show all transactions where you paid for print advertising and online advertising. This comes in handy when I go to the accountant to do my taxes because I simply print out a Profit-and-Loss report and my accountant has all he needs to do my taxes quickly.

You can see in these programs whether you are making a profit and how much. You can easily tell how much you are spending and on what kinds of things, such as rent, office supplies, postage, advertising, and so on. You can then manage your costs more effectively by knowing where to cut, where to spend more, and learn whether your income allows your business to be self-sustaining.

Customer Database

LISA Don't be scared by the word "database." A database is just a way to store information in an organized manner. If you have an address book or just a list of names, email addresses, and phone numbers you have a database.

As a small business you will want to keep track of who came to investigate or buy your product or services, customers' history of doing business with you, and the last time a customer visited your business. This way you can determine which customers are your most frequent buyers, and, as we will discuss in Chapter 6, this is important, because those who buy from you will more likely buy again.

The better you know your customer the easier it is for you to build a relationship. Businesses call this Customer Relationship Management (CRM) and the computer program used for this is called a Customer Relationship Management System.

Your Computer's Customer Database

CINDY   As your number of clients increase, it's important to find a way to easily keep track of names, emails, addresses and transactions. There are multiple online and in-house databases. I have an extensive customer database of over 7,000 clients and students, so when I need to find all who live in Texas, I cannot look though each record to find them. I need a database with a strong search capability.

Being a little old-fashioned, I still like to send my best clients Christmas cards, and so I have my clients' addresses as well as email information. Being that I am a numerologist as well as psychic, I also have clients' birthdays. When I have an assistant, I send out actual birthday cards. I can't tell you how excited my clients are to actually get a card in the mail rather than an email.

As you can imagine, regular mail can be expensive, so I make sure to make any mailing a marketing opportunity. I include holiday gift ideas for my products and services in my early Christmas card and a discount coupon in my birthday cards. I don't send out 7,000 Christmas cards, rather, I search my database to find out which clients have had two or more sessions in the previous year or bought multiple products and only send them the "snail mail" version of my Christmas card.

The rest of my clients get emails with my Holiday wish and specials. You can see why it is important to have a searchable database as well as the ability to make address labels. Handwriting 300+ Christmas cards would be a challenge! More and more I rely on emails for my marketing, which are more financially rewarding for most marketing opportunities.

A good database will also allow you to see where your marketing does the most good. If it is simply to ask your new clients, "How did you hear of me?" you can track the response in your Customer database and at the end of the year, or the quarter, pull a report. You will be able to see if your website, your emails, your paid advertising, or word of mouth is your best advertising tool.

This type of information is invaluable and almost impossible to mine without a good database. When first starting out, you might choose to keep your clients' data in a spreadsheet. There is nothing wrong with this, but as your business matures, you will find a spreadsheet clumsy. But a spreadsheet is better than a file box or names on sheets of paper.

When you are looking for a good database, here are some must-have features:

- SEARCHABLE: You must be able to search by almost all, if not all of the fields in the customer database.
- LABEL-MAKING CAPABILITIES: You may not send out mailings often, but you want the capability.
- MULTIPLE FIELDS: You need more than name and address, you may want birthday or when the client's last session was. You may want to note which product or service the client uses the most.
- CUSTOMIZABLE FIELDS: Your business is unique and having customizable fields for your data is key to making your customer database work best for you.
- ACCESSIBILITY: This may not be a big issue at first, but if you travel for business or pleasure, you may want access to your customer database when you are out of your office.
- SECURITY: Your clients' private information is sacred. It is important you respect that.

Security is especially important if you handle credit cards; security then becomes a legal issue. I have clients who don't want to give me their credit card information each time we have a session and have asked me to keep it "on file." I don't keep any credit card information on the computer. I use an old-fashioned card file system, which I don't leave lying around. More and more, with online payment companies like PayPal, I won't need my client's credit card information to get paid.

LISA In general, after you have used a customer's credit card and the transaction is completed, you probably should not keep credit card information on file. Keeping credit card numbers opens you up to a liability problem if there is any credit card fraud with that number. Online credit card processing services protect you from this because they do not store the credit card numbers. Thus, it would be better to use an online service like PayPal.

CINDY You will always be updating your technology and exploring new and better ways to operate your business. The customer database program that you buy today may be outdated tomorrow. Be sure to put aside money for updating computer programs or you will feel unable to explore new options that can make your life easier as your business grows.

My database is perhaps the only aspect of my business that I've had trouble with in finding a good "Mac computer software" option. I spent quite a bit on my customer database program for Mac and I had to pay for help from the One to One service at the Apple Store to actually build my program. It works for now, but if a better online customer database program comes up, I know I can afford to investigate it because I keep money aside for this type of situation.

My business is growing; my needs are shifting. If a new product would work better with my new business complexities, then I need to see if my new business income supports the cost of the new customer database service. I will weigh cost with efficiency and make the decision. It is a constant dance between the old ways and the new ways and spending every penny you have on a new product for your business because you think it will last you ten years is unrealistic.

We will discuss the idea of having a replacement budget, or what I call the "Oh No!" fund, at the end of this chapter.

Online Customer Database

LISA An email marketing program is a good way to keep track of customers, particularly for me, as an email address is usually the first piece of information I get from a potential customer. Most email marketing programs have all the initial fields for information you want to keep and you can add fields for other information you want to track.

I will break out my customers in subgroups based on how they came to me, what course they've taken with me, or what product they've bought from me. This provides a way to look up a customer and see what his or her history is with my business. I can also use an email marketing system to "segment" my customers into groups and then send out a specific email to only one group from the entire list.

This is convenient, especially if you don't want to bombard your entire list with lots of emails. Email marketing systems are so smart now that you can send to varied segments, such as, only to customers who have opened your email in the past six months, or who have opened your email the most, or even to those who are located in a particular area of the world.

An online customer or CRM database that small businesses can use free is called Zoho CRM. I have it synchronized with my email marketing program, which is MailChimp, so the email address are the same in each. You do not have to get this fancy, and can easily use an address book that comes with your computer, such as "Contacts" on the Apple Mac.

Two additional categories of information I keep in my customer database are how clients found me, for example, did they sign up on my website or at one of my lectures, and where they spent money with me, for example, was it at a course I gave or a private session, etc. Many online CRM databases are available, and they range from simple to complex. Most of them are used to track the sales process.

Reliable Transportation

`CINDY` A reliable car or other transportation is essential when starting a business. If you live in a city environment, being on a good bus, subway or train line is important. Much of your marketing will be done out of the office. If you can't get to your clients or they can't get to you, your spiritual business won't be able to go anywhere … literally.

The "Oh No" Fund

`CINDY` Assume that you have your business up and running: you have a relatively new computer, a good car, and you plan to do a lot of holistic events within a day's drive from your home. Now it is three years later, and you have put an extra 10,000 miles each year on your car, so your pretty new car now has 55,000 miles and you need new tires, brakes, and a tune-up. Plus, your computer is five years old and starting to slow down running all the new programs for your business.

Using pretend numbers, you know that in the next few months you'll need $1,000 for a new computer (triple that if you want a Mac), you need $800 for tires, and say another $500 for the car repairs. You also know that your car will need to be replaced in another few years. "Oh No!" Where are you going to come up with the $2,300 for the immediate stuff and double that much for the down payment on a new car in a few years?

This is where your spiritual business can get into trouble, by not planning ahead. If you started your Oh No! fund when you first started the business, you would have that money waiting. If you had only added $65 a month, you would already have $2,340! You may have extra expenses beyond these, which is why I recommend you put twice that much away each month. But you get the idea.

Considering how long computers last or quickly become obsolete, you probably need to plan on a new computer every three to five years. Other things to consider are how much are you printing and how many pages do you get per ink cartridge? How much does your accountant cost? How much is your rent going up next year? It isn't just things that need to be replaced, services go up and big bills like car tires or other emergencies can be prepared for with a good Oh No! fund balance.

Of course, you can't plan for everything, but you can at least be prepared for most expenses. I suggest everyone have an Oh No! fund for their home expenses, too, yet having one for your business will allow you to just slow down, not have to stop, when you hit those financial bumps in the road.

You now have everything you need financially to succeed. In the next few chapters, you will learn marketing techniques that will help you attract clients, resonate with them, and then turn them into long-time customers using synergizing techniques.

CHAPTER FIVE

Marketing Your Spiritual Business – ATTRACT!

· · · · · · · · · · · · · · ·

SPIRITUAL BUSINESS TIP #14

Marketing your spiritual business allows your potential customers to get to know you.

LISA   Marketing your spiritual business is all about your potential customers getting to know you and what your services are. By marketing, people who need your services can find you. Many times people who are just starting their spiritual business shy away from marketing because they feel it's all about the hard sell, but it's not, really. It is about the Law of Attraction, attracting those customers who are already seeking you, then connecting with them by forming a relationship, and finally deepening that relationship.

Attracting customers is the same process as making new friends, or starting a romantic relationship. In this metaphor, you start out by looking for a person who seems like he or she would make a good friend or romantic partner.

The scenario would go something like this: You see someone that you are attracted to, you introduce yourself and make small talk to see if you have things in common. As you learn more about each other you both may move to the next step of going out for coffee or lunch together, or the classic "go out for a drink."

As you talk you might find you have similar interests and discover you both enjoy the same things. You begin to realize that you like being with the other person and want to spend even more time together. You might go to the movies or spend an afternoon at the museum. As time goes on you eventually commit to a longer relationship, like "going steady," or even marriage.

You may not realize it, but customers look for a spiritual service provider in the same way. Let's look at it from their point of view. As a customer, you start by looking for a service provider that you are attracted to, someone who provides the things you're interested in and does things the way you like.

You do some research and come across marketing material, which might be a website or brochure about the provider's services. You investigate further by taking a free class, a free consultation session, or perhaps read a book or article he or she has written. You begin to develop a rapport with the person, perhaps having a short discussion after a lecture, or listening to a talk. This is the beginning of your relationship.

If you feel comfortable and like what you see and hear, you take the next step to purchase the service or product. Usually you buy a smaller service to test the waters; but if you resonate strongly with someone you may jump in and buy a bigger package. This is sort of the "love at first sight" scenario.

Eventually, you buy larger services or more expensive products. As your relationship grows, you become a regular customer, coming back over and over again. That is a committed relationship, or what we in business call customer loyalty.

These steps can be broken down into three areas: attracting, resonating and synergizing. (1) Attract your customer by making your introduction or getting him or her to notice you. (2) See if the prospective client resonates with you and your work by allowing her to try out your service or product. And finally, (3) synergize with the client's needs and wants with your services and products thereby building customer loyalty. In this way, we can break down spiritual marketing as: Attract, Resonate, and Synergize.

> **SPIRITUAL BUSINESS TIP #15**
>
> Spiritual Marketing can be broken out into three areas:
> Attracting, Resonating and Synergizing

CINDY Almost everyone who is starting a spiritual business began as an interested seeker looking for spiritual services. It is critical to remember that marketing is not an imposition or invasion, it is a way to serve an existing need. When you were first starting out you probably wished there were better websites, free programs, and introductory specials out there.

Why should it be a negative situation or an imposition to let people know you are offering the same thing you were searching for a few years ago or may still be looking for? I have not learned everything there is to know or tried every spiritual business out there, so I am sure anyone reading this book is just as excited to know about a coupon or a free talk about a subject they want to investigate.

So don't be afraid to put the word out, or even shout out about what you are offering. Think of good marketing as an additional service you offer.

THE SPIRITUAL LAW OF ATTRACTION FOR MARKETING – "GETTING TO KNOW YOU"

Why Attract and Market?

LISA Quite simply, if you don't market your business to your prospective clients, they have no way of knowing who you are, what you offer, and how they can benefit from your business. It then helps to activate the Law of Attraction by setting your intention. Marketing is letting people know what you are offering. To be successful in helping people find your spiritual business, it is your responsibility to reach out and let them know what you offer and that you exist!

The spiritual Law of Attraction is your way of connecting and reaching out to your prospective clients. As the Law of Attraction states, what you think about is what you will receive. When you have the intention to attract and draw clients to you who are looking for your services, those thoughts are stored energetically, in escrow if you will, to bring them to you.

In a way, you can think of your clients as waiting for you energetically and marketing just helps them get to you. Marketing is putting the spiritual Law of Attraction into action to connect you with your customer by you doing the work.

The main steps of the Law of Attraction are:

- Set Your Intention – Be clear on what you want and see it as already yours.
- Act – Take action steps to move towards your intended goal.
- Let Go – Let the Universe bring it to you.

Marketing your business means taking action steps to let people know who you are and what you do in a way that allows them to find you! *Attract* is the first step in the Attract, Resonate, Synergize marketing process. There are many traditional and exciting new methods to attract and find a match between your work and your customer. We'll go over each of these.

CINDY In using the Law of Attraction, realize that your emotional and mental states will attract the same energy. For example, if you are down or frustrated about your business not taking off, you may find that you begin to attract clients who have similar issues. It is a good idea to examine the energy of the clients you are attracting to make sure you are putting forth the best energy possible.

Sometimes a cigar is just a cigar and you'll have a grumpy client, but if there is a frequent pattern to the type of clients you are attracting, examine yourself. I know when I am having a difficult time in my life I have fewer clients. It is as if the Universe doesn't want me to work with people unless I am in a positive headspace. Those clients who are sensitive to energy will sense an imbalance in yours and just might not show up. You are in a spiritual business and you are likely to have clients that may not be consciously aware of your energy but can sense if you are not putting forth positive and healthy vibrations.

I have also found that if I look at my client and see a dollar sign, that client doesn't return. I think they truly sense that your underlying motivation is not being of service to him or her; it is being of service to your bank account. That is why it is so important to maintain an outside income until your business has supported itself for at least a year. That way you are not putting out "poverty consciousness" energy. Clients don't mind you making money, but they may pick up and react poorly to the "poverty energy" you are putting out.

LISA I agree with Cindy. I found that when I decided I wanted to attract only students willing to pay for classes that I charged more for, I was actually able to fill classes with higher prices. In fact, at the same time some of the classes I taught almost for free began to lose students.

What to Market?

LISA You may be asking, what should I market? The answer is: YOU. The first thing in any small business is to market yourself as a practitioner or as the person selling a product. Your potential customers are going to want to know why they should come to you. They'll want to see what makes you different from others.

People want to know who they are getting their services from, so it is important to show why you are just the right person to help them. Here is where it is important to be authentic, not just when you serve, but also in your marketing. People want to see you, as you are, not someone you think you should be.

CINDY I find that clients often form an opinion of me by looking at my picture, not if I am fat or thin, but if I look approachable and welcoming. Also, they seem to be attracted to how I connect to them in a familiar and casual way on my website. I am careful not to use slang or be unprofessional in marketing, though I want the reader to see who I am.

On my website, I include pictures of me on my travels to give them a feel of what experiences I have had and what interests me. Let people in and they will come in.

LISA Market the results people will gain, not the details of your service or product. It is important to tell people in your marketing how you are going to help transform their lives, where you will take them. This is not what you are going to do or what you are going to give them, but rather how they will benefit from your service directly.

For example, a spiritual business that helps people reduce stress and gain mental clarity through meditation is going to transform people who are anxious, stressed, and harried into someone who is calmer, more centered and effective in life, which can lead to more happiness and accomplishment.

CINDY The point Lisa made is one I often forget to do. I become more tied up in writing about the service instead of how the client will benefit! I can see how much better the effects are when I focus on results rather than process. When customers can appreciate how they will benefit, you will not only connect your service with their needs, but they will also better understand your focus and strengths.

How to ATTRACT Through Marketing

LISA The first step in attracting is to set your intention and state your desire. Attracting is not sleazy pushing or manipulation that people associate with selling. In fact, selling, by definition, is simply "telling someone the merits of something." Your desire is to connect with people who want services or products that will help them transform their lives, or at least a part of their lives. You can state your affirmation: *"I see and draw to me the perfect customers and clients who need and want my services/products now."*

The second step is to put your intention into action. As the story goes, there was a gentleman who asked God, "I pray to you every night that I win the lottery, and I haven't won! Why are my prayers not working?" God replies, "Help me out a little, go buy a ticket." You need to take action so the Universe can bring you what you desire.

You put that intention into action by helping people know what you have to offer and where to find you. That is advertising. Advertising is an excellent way to start taking action, and now, with Internet marketing, you can easily afford advertising that is highly effective.

Whether you use the Internet or not, the best way to begin advertising is to go local. This means start where you live or where your business is located physically. You can advertise four different ways: in-person appearances, print and online ads, radio and TV/video traditionally or online, and partnerships.

Don't worry about doing all of these, just start with one or two you are comfortable with. We'll go over each so you can see how it's done and what is most effective.

Reaching More People to Attract Through Advertising

SPIRITUAL BUSINESS TIP #16

Now with the Internet you can advertise inexpensively and reach a very targeted market.

LISA Advertising is a simple and easy way to reach many people. Now, with the Internet, you can advertise inexpensively and reach a targeted market. Traditional advertising, as in print media, is also effective and can be worth it in the long run. It is important to keep in mind that advertising is a way to stay in front of your customer or your potential customer, to remind them that you are there and active.

It often takes many times of seeing an ad before a customer actually picks up the phone or takes action to buy your services or products. Just think of how many times you have seen an ad or the name of someone before you decided to buy a product or service. The more your name is in front of someone the more likely he or she will be interested in doing business with you.

One of the best things I ever heard at one of my events was from someone telling me she'd seen my name everywhere. I knew then that my marketing was working. You may want to make sure that your advertising budget is affordable and maintainable.

Another thing to remember is that every time you do an event, put on a class, offer your services somewhere, or speak publicly, it is a form of advertising for you. I have found that the more events I do, the more it generates interest from people asking what else I have to offer.

If you have other services, products, or items that people can purchase or buy, be ready to present those or have information on hand about them to share. I always try to bring postcards and flyers of other services I have to offer when I do an event just in case there is interest. Even if people don't ask directly about other things you do, you can always mention them.

Paid Advertising That Is Worth It!

LISA As much as you may be resistant to advertising, don't be. Advertising really does bring in business even though you don't see immediate results. In addition, advertising online is much cheaper than print advertising and you can reach more people around the world. On Facebook, you can advertise for as little as $1 or $2 a day, up to thousands of dollars a day.

You can also target who sees your advertising in ways you could never do with print advertising, which greatly increases the chances that you will get a customer from your ad. You can use the Internet to advertise easily on social media platforms and reach thousands of people that you could never reach affordably through print media. I used to pay between $400 and $500 for a monthly ad, which included a "News Brief," in a local free magazine that served my target market.

Now I'm finding that Facebook is more effective for driving people to my website and eventually purchasing my products, because the ads can target potential customers who are even more closely aligned with my services and products.

CINDY Advertising can be very expensive and a prospective client needs to see an ad about six times in a row to actually call. Running an ad only one time is a waste of money. Spend your advertising dollar wisely. Think about advertising costs in relation to how many sessions or products you would need to sell to pay for the ad. Currently I advertise in a monthly local spiritual/holistic magazine and it costs me $25 a month. That is $300 a year. Calculating my least expensive offering at the time of this writing, I need to make about 7 sales per year to break even.

If a person books a longer reading that cuts down the number of readings I need to pay for the ad. Since I usually do a longer session, I figure I need about 4 sales a year to pay for that ad. I get more than that, but it is not consistent. That's why figuring it yearly or even over six months is better as I don't get a reading every month out of that particular ad.

ATTRACT - ONLINE WITH SOCIAL MEDIA AND NETWORKING

LISA Almost everyone has some sort of electronic device that can communicate with the Internet, such as a smartphone, an electronic tablet and of course the computer. People are now addicted to their electronic devices and are always using them, so connecting with your potential customers and developing relationships with them is now easier than ever before. You can attract with Internet Marketing easily through social media websites where people "gather," such as Facebook, MeetUp, LinkedIn, and others.

There are always new social networking sites and those that fade in popularity, so it is important to stay current on social networking trends.

CINDY For any type of social networking, it is important to keep your "page" active. Even if you simply post a pretty picture with a spiritual saying on it, it is better than a stagnant page. If you find you can't post at least once every few days, it is better to take down the page. People want to engage and know you are available. Stagnant pages show that you aren't engaged or don't care. This may not be the case, you may just be incredibly busy, yet it is important to set aside time to post on your page.

Today you can use sites like Hootsuite or Facebook that feature a "scheduling" option that allows you to pre-post and schedule for a future date. You can do a week's worth of posting at one sitting and schedule it so it looks like you're online all day, every day.

It is just as important to avoid overposting. If someone's feed is filled with your posts daily, they may block you. I know I have blocked people who post every 10 minutes. If you have a lot of exciting things to say, use the scheduler and space them out.

Also, with social networking, make sure that your posts are set as "public," rather than only seen by friends. You want people to be able to re-post your postings, and if you set your security or privacy too high it will eliminate the chance of a post going viral! Because you are making your posts public, be careful about what you say. If you need to make a political statement, rant, or talk about personal issues, you may want to send an email or just post to a specific group of people.

LISA Social media sites, such as Facebook, YouTube, Twitter, and LinkedIn, are popular places to advertise because it is inexpensive and can reach many people.

You can create a Facebook Page, which is different from a Facebook Personal profile, for free. A Facebook Page is essentially a free profile for a business. You can then create a Facebook advertisement for your Facebook Page or for your website. You cannot create a Facebook advertisement on your Facebook Personal profile. Facebook advertising to get more "Likes" for your page is very powerful. The more you post, the more those who liked your page will engage with you. Engaging with customers through Facebook is another part of Internet marketing.

Facebook advertising is very affordable and extremely powerful. The best thing about Facebook is that you can target your advertising to specific groups of people, that is, the demographics. For example, if you would like to reach only women between the ages of 35 and 65, who are interested in yoga, also like Pilates, and live in California you can set up your Facebook ads to only show up on the pages of people who fit that criteria. Generally, it is much more difficult to do that with snail-mail advertising.

CINDY It is a frustrating fact that everything you post on Facebook does not show up on everyone else's feed. What you see on your Facebook feed depends on what posts you interact with by "liking" the post or sharing it. If you don't "Like" or Share a post from a particular page, eventually you won't see posts from that page anymore.

Occasionally run a campaign that gives something to your Facebook followers for liking or sharing your post. You could give away a free session or perhaps a free meditation you have recorded. It doesn't matter what you give away, it is just important that it is valuable enough to tempt someone to like or share your post. Not only will this ensure that the followers continue to see what you post, but if they share the post, all of their friends will see it, too!

I did this when we published *Soul Soothers*. We had a contest for five free, signed copies of the book and if you shared the post, which was about

Soul Soothers, you were entered into the drawing for a free book. We received a lot of free publicity for the book and it just cost us five books and shipping!

There are pros and cons to the business Facebook Page in which someone likes the page versus a Personal Facebook page in which you need to "Friend" the person. There is no right or wrong choice between the Facebook formats, but if you like to do events, you might want to think about a Personal Facebook page. If someone "Likes" your page, you cannot invite him or her to an event. This became an issue when events became a more popular and excellent marketing tool.

I still have two pages, yet I invited all of my Facebook business page people to friend me on my personal page. Now I have to be more careful what I put on my personal page. I have had people tell me they enjoy following me as I travel around the world, and they keep an eye out for my posts.

Even my personal vacations have become an excellent marketing tool. I make sure to post content on both pages, and this is where using Hootsuite to schedule your posts is helpful. I avoid posting the same content on both pages because the pages share readers.

One more thing about Facebook and other social networking sites: keep the vibration of the posts positive. Yes, you may have had a tough day and want to rant or complain, but if you have clients looking at your page, talk to a friend instead. Also, ask family and friends to avoid tagging you on embarrassing, political, or other posts you don't want seen by the public.

This is a good idea even if you don't have a public persona, but especially for the spiritual business practitioner. Bottom line, if you want to promote a post, a business Facebook page works well. If you want to invite people to events, a personal page works better. This is why I've kept both going.

LISA YouTube allows you to put links in your video so you can direct traffic to any web page you'd like. At the time of this writing, these features are free. While YouTube does not allow you to post videos that are pure advertising, you can post a video and have links in your video that go to your website. You also can put links to your website in the description of your video or create a YouTube ad and pay them to show your ad to YouTube viewers. You can target your audience with YouTube, which allows you to be seen by certain demographics, locations, and even suggest other videos to place your ad on. The main difference between Facebook and YouTube is that ads on YouTube tend to be more often a video and a link, instead of text or image with a link to a video or website.

Twitter can also be a useful place to post. Using under 140 characters, post a short promotional line with a link to your website, blog, or wherever you would like to send people.

CINDY Twitter can be a great outlet for marketing. You can post links, pictures, and content. It does take work to get followers, yet my husband, David Bennett, has about 45,000 followers and he has turned his tweets into a strong marketing tool.

He rarely puts marketing-type tweets on his feed. Using a social media scheduler, every day he enters about 20 posts. Most are what he calls reflections, spiritual thoughts he's gotten during meditation, and maybe two or so of the 20 tweets have marketing content.

If you only use Twitter for marketing, you will struggle to get followers. As in emails, use Twitter to let people know who you are. Tweet content that people want to see. Also, a tweet has a lifetime of about 20 minutes. In other words, after 20 minutes, your tweet is so far down in the feed that it is rarely seen unless someone goes searching for you specifically. This is why Dave puts out about 20 a day. Facebook posts have a longer lifetime, yet you can get more followers with Twitter.

LISA LinkedIn is a directory of people's professional profiles, which is a nice way to share your business and educational background. It has become a popular networking site where professionals connect for business.

A simple listing on LinkedIn is free. There are also networking groups on LinkedIn and you can post work status changes in your profile just as in Facebook.

As the Internet evolves there will be more and more ways to advertise using text, video, links, audio and you will find that platforms, such as Facebook, Twitter and YouTube will start to expand and overlap in types of advertising choices.

Websites – Global Advertising and #1 in Internet Marketing

SPIRITUAL BUSINESS TIP #17

Your website doesn't have to be fancy, but it should have information about you and your services or products.

LISA In the old days, when you started your business you "hung out your shingle," meaning you put up a sign outside your building to show you were in business. In this way, anyone passing by would know you are open for business. Years later you would list your business in the Yellow Pages, and anyone in the local area could see you there, reaching a slightly larger audience for your services..

Today, your "shingle" is a website. A website is a must-have for any business because people are so accustomed to searching on the Internet to find out more about a business.

A website is now very easy to create and it can be done for very low cost, or no cost. You can put out a lot more information about yourself and your business than you could in the phone book or on a shingle! It is an exciting time for you to be in business for yourself.

SPIRITUAL BUSINESS TIP #18

A website is a "must have" for any business.

LISA With a website you can reach people globally, spreading the word about your services and products more powerfully than ever. I have clients from around the world, on every continent and have had students travel across the country and come from other countries to take my classes. It always surprises me how the Internet can make us all get to know each other and feel so close, even though we are thousands of miles apart.

Before you get tense, especially if you are not technical, don't worry! If you can type an email, you can build a website — it is that easy and getting easier. If you really don't want to do it yourself, there are plenty of services and freelancers out there who will do it for you. Websites are here to stay for a while, and they will evolve to being simpler to create and more beautiful to look at. It is worthwhile to invest in one, and you don't have to spend that much money.

SPIRITUAL BUSINESS TIP #19

A stagnant website site is invisible; you need to update it regularly.

LISA Let's assume you are ready to create your website, or have someone do it for you. There are good websites and bad ones. What are the essential things you need on a website to attract your customers? Because your website is your home base, it is where you want to send everyone to get to know you. There are three essential pieces of information you must have on your website: a description of what it is you do to transform people through your service or product results, who you are and why you do what you do, and how you connect with customers.

Let's first go through how to create your website to attract prospective customers. You'll want to keep your website simple and easy for people to get the information they are looking for quickly. As a person or practitioner, you must be authentic, relatable and accessible. That should be easy for you, as a spiritual business entrepreneur, because all you need to do is present yourself with your heart.

Being open and authentic shines through in how you describe yourself and your business. Your mission is to help others with an open heart. People will naturally be attracted to you, because an open heart is very attractive! Keep this in mind as you create content for your website. Let the client know what you do and how you transform people.

What you do to transform people's lives is the result of your services, whatever these might be. People want to know what you will do for them and how it will change their lives, or make their lives better. Describe not what you do or how you do it, but what you can do for others and what your services or product will do for them. If you were selling drill bits, people don't want to hear what those drill bits are made of, they want to know how great a hole they'll make!

On your home page describe your services or products in terms of how people can benefit from them. How you actually perform your service or how your product works can be described later, because it is secondary. How you can help people and transform their lives should be on the website's home page, to be seen right away.

The second thing that should be on your website is something about you. It doesn't have to be long, just an introduction to who you are. You can put this on the home page or on a separate "About" page. You want people to readily relate to you and feel comfortable about you. This is where you begin to build your relationship, the "attraction" part.

Writing about yourself is best done in the first person, particularly in spiritual businesses, where people want to relate to another person, not an impersonal figure or company. It's very important to be likeable and relatable. This is something that I needed to work on, and some of you may have to as well, if you come from the corporate or academic world.

I was very used to writing in the third person and in an official sounding and impersonal way. That approach doesn't resonate with people and certainly is harder to attract others with. First person sounds like you're speaking with your audience directly.

Here is an example "About page" from my website written in first person:

> *"I'm Lisa K., creator of Developing Your Intuition, a system that helps people master their intuition so they can draw on it when they want, with detail and clarity on anything they want to use it for. Many of my students have successfully used their intuition to help with decisions in their daily life to manifesting more abundance and an ability to receive inner wisdom.*
>
> *I developed my own intuition to the point where it has led me to amazing results including saving my life. I am always comforted knowing I can rely on my inner guidance by knowing how it works, and how to tap into it when and on what I want. As a popular intuitive consultant, I am often sold out at public events."*

CINDY Here's an example of the importance of a website for any business. When we were looking for house contractors, we went to the local Home Builders Association's website for referrals. The only people we even considered were contractors with a website. We picked our contractor because his website gave insight into him and his projects. It was the ability to make a connection before we called that gave him our business, and we were surely not alone here.

We have been loyal customers ever since. This experience showed me how important marketing is in giving you insight into the owner of a business.

LISA Cindy's experience is a good indicator of how important it is to have a website these days. People are going less and less to the phone book, if at all. You don't have to create a complex website, a single page is a good place to start. Have enough information there for people to know who you are, what you do, and how to contact you. That's all you need.

As technology evolves it will become easier and easier to put together a web site or improve your "Internet presence." Even if you are not technical, you can now easily be out there on the Internet.

ATTRACT – TRADITIONALLY

In-Person Appearances

SPIRITUAL BUSINESS TIP #20

In-person appearances can be very powerful in allowing people to get to know you.

LISA In-person appearances are very powerful in reaching people and allowing them to get to know you. It is also a traditional way that small businesses and practitioners have been getting their name out to the public for years. Some of the things you can do in person are to give a lecture or seminar, or offer samples of your services or products.

Places where you can give in-person talks would be local metaphysical stores, bookstores, health and wellness fairs, as well as a public or private event. If you feel uncomfortable giving a talk or speech, you could demonstrate your services. For example, if you offer intuitive readings you might want to do an event reading for people at a discounted rate.

This way people can sample your services at a lower price to see if they like what it is you offer. Make sure to be clear that they are getting your service at a discounted rate. You could also give them a smaller discount in the form of a coupon for their next reading. At metaphysical stores, health and wellness fairs, or similar events, often you can teach a class or give a lecture. You can partner with metaphysical stores or holistic wellness centers to put on a class, and they will take a portion of what the students pay to cover rent and any advertising they do for you. This is also a great way to build your client list and reach people who are looking for your kind of service. Usually these stores or centers have their own customer list, which they will advertise to. It is well worth the portion of money they take to host your event.

CINDY The percentage the store or event takes vary in these circumstances. Often it ranges from the store taking 20 to 40 percent of the class fee. Some places will charge a flat fee for the room. Make sure to find out what advertising they will do and what they expect from you. Don't depend on the store to bring in the people; it is a two-way street as the store or center will want you to bring new customers to them, too!

LISA Expos are also great places to reach new clients. Expos take place throughout the year in the same location and often attract a large group of people. The wonderful thing about these events is that they bring in a very targeted group of people that fit your market.

These events have two kinds of sections. One is for speakers or lecturers and the other is for exhibitors. Some specialized expos will have an additional section for intuitive readers and/or healers. As with metaphysical centers, some expos will take a cut of whatever the customer pays for in exchange for allowing you to give your healing or do a reading. Most often you will need to pay them if you wish to speak or give a lecture. You may also need to pay them for an exhibitor's table, which sometimes includes advertising for your service in their brochures or online, or may include a speaker spot.

If an expo does not have a special section for intuitive readers you can read at an exhibitor table, which you rent. This has its pros and cons. The pro being that you have an exhibitor table for your other products and you gain more visibility; the con is that it's often noisy in the exhibitor hall.

CINDY Yes, this type of environment is noisy and there are booth fees or percentages to be paid to the promoter, yet an expo or fair is one of the best ways to reach a targeted audience. Check with the promoter as to fees, types of booths, and what is acceptable as far as marketing techniques.

In Upstate New York, there is usually no fee for giving a lecture if you are one of the vendors or practitioners, yet it is rare to see an "information only" table at a psychic fair. Information tables are more common at Health Fairs, although sometimes the promoter will not allow you to offer free mini sessions if it competes with a vendor or practitioner who is charging for a similar service. It simply is a matter of checking with the promoter of the event to know the rules.

Holistic or Spiritual Magazines

CINDY With local holistic or spiritual magazines, it makes sense to advertise whenever you publish an article in one. I have found that local magazines offer the best bang for my advertising buck. Plus, you look more professional and educated on your topic after writing an article that gets published!

LISA I agree with Cindy that holistic or spiritual magazines are one of the best places to advertise. These magazines have a targeted market that falls in line with spiritual businesses. Their readership is most likely interested in the kind of services you provide. If you were to advertise in more general magazines or newspapers, most of the readers will probably not be interested in spiritual businesses.

Normally, if you advertise in one of these holistic or spiritual magazines, they will also publish an article by you. These articles are often written as a "News Brief" and are more informative rather than an advertisement and is considered an article for specifically announcing news. The great thing about News Briefs is that they also serve as an indirect form of marketing.

Remember, the idea is to reach people who are specifically interested in your kind of service and let them know about you. If you do not want to spend a lot of money with a big advertisement in these magazines, you can list a calendar event for one of your programs free or a very small fee.

Many holistic or spiritual magazines and newspapers are now published on the Internet, and some are only published online. They provide the same kinds of articles, advertisements, and information you find in print. Many times the cost for advertising online in these magazines is cheaper than in their printed version and can be beneficial for businesses that do not require a customer to be physically present. Holistic and spiritual magazines and newspapers are ways to advertise and reach a new audience inexpensively.

CINDY With online magazines you, as an author, usually don't know how many people are actually reading the articles. Sometimes you can get the demographics by clicking "data" in the magazine's advertising media kit. Some online magazines like OMTimes have an extensive readership, yet not all do. But how many people read the online magazine isn't all that important, because if you have your social networking set up, you can post the link to your article there.

Writing articles definitely puts you a step up in your industry and with your clients. Make sure the articles are interesting, informative, and inspiring, not an infomercial. You want to present real quality information. Always ask a friend to proofread it for you. Typos can ruin even the best information by making you look careless and sloppy.

Phone Book Advertising

CINDY Phone book advertising is a thing of the past. I had an ad in my local phone book for over twenty years. Now with a good website and Internet presence, I don't need it. Also, if you decide to put an ad in a phone book, you are locked into a one-year contract. But if you do take an ad, note that you can often negotiate your phone book advertising bill after a few years.

Newspaper Advertising

CINDY I used to advertise in my local "Pennysaver" which has now gone out of business. I found it was a waste of money as the people who read the "discount papers" were usually only looking for a discount. I got people looking for the five-dollar readings. Yet, if I have a good special offer, I might consider a discount paper to get my name out.

Newspaper advertisements are often expensive, but if you have a local newspaper, and you place an occasional ad, you might find that they are more likely to do an article on your business. I have had good luck when they do a local business card directory, which is a page of local business cards without additional ad copy. If you are fortunate enough to get an article written about you, your accomplishments, or your business, then invest in a bigger ad that week and maybe the next few weeks after.

Remember, it doesn't pay to buy an ad just once in a newspaper. If you do not have name recognition, people need to see an ad at least six times to act on it.

Radio and TV/Video Traditionally or Online

LISA Traditionally, radio and television was the way to advertise a business. When you're first starting out, local radio or television stations might be interested doing a story on your new business. They are often looking for good local stories for their viewers or listeners. Usually this is in the form of an interview.

With the Internet, many online radio shows and social media video sites are available. Online video show hosts who have their own show channel may be interested in having you as a guest on the show. Thousands of amateur and professional radio show hosts online are always looking for guests to be on their show. You can search for a show that complements your kind of business. YouTube, Vimeo and Ustream are popular places where people have posted videos on their own show channel.

Show hosts look for thought-provoking guests with a topic that is interesting to their listeners or viewers. It is important that you listen to their previous shows to see if you fit the profile of a guest who is right for their show. Keep in mind that hosts get many requests by strangers to be on their shows, so you'll have to stand out among the crowd.

The way you stand out among the crowd is to be prepared to show how your topic is going to be a good fit and how it will benefit the show's listeners or viewers. Both Cindy and I have hosted our own radio shows for many years. One thing I tell potential guests is that our show is not meant to be an hour-long advertisement for their products. Our show is to educate, entertain, and provide useful information for our listeners. So be prepared for other show hosts to be looking for the same.

CINDY Keep in mind that you can post a link of the radio or video show on your social networking sites, so don't worry if the show does not have a large audience. Sometimes a host gets off topic or a lot of commercials interrupt the flow of what I am trying to get across during an interview.

So, I often edit my interviews before I post them. Another thing you can do with the radio or video interviews is to create short one-to-two-minute snippets for social media, because many listeners will only listen to a short segment. Most people don't have an hour to spend listening to you.

On my Mac I use GarageBand and iMovie for my editing. Then I use free software that I got online, called Podsnack, to turn my short audio segments into a link that can be embedded on my website or posted on my social networking. These free software options change all the time, so search for "HTML audio player" to see what is available.

LISA One of the most popular free programs for the Mac or PC for audio recording and editing is Audacity. Audacity is quite powerful and fairly easy to use. It has been around for over a decade and is still one of the most downloaded free software programs available. It has a large set of editing and mixing features.

Now that you have attracted prospective clients and have them interested in your services, let's discover how to resonate with them so that they want to continue to work with you and explore your full range of services or products.

CHAPTER SIX

Spiritual Sales and Building Your Tribe – RESONATE!

· · · · · · · · · · · · · · · ·

STARTING TO BUILD YOUR CUSTOMER TRIBE

SPIRITUAL BUSINESS TIP #21

When people resonate with who you are they will spend more time with you.

LISA Building a following of raving fans and loyal customers is important to keep your business going. Those committed customers are the ones who will come back and spread the word about your business. Customers who have been with you longer and trust you and your work will also be willing to go the extra mile and make the deeper commitment.

This means they are more likely to spend a weekend or even week-long retreat with you, pay more for personalized services, and want more of what you have to offer. When people resonate with who you are and what you do, they will spend more time with you. They become your "customer tribe" who are now your loyal customers. How do you motivate people who are attracted to your business into becoming loyal customers? You give them an opportunity to resonate with you.

Say you've attracted a new set of people to your business; they are just becoming interested in you and haven't yet bought anything, or may have bought something small from you. This is a wonderful group of self-selected highly interested potential customers. Something in them has already begun to resonate with you and your business.

After you have attracted your new or potentially new customer, you must build on this connection to keep them coming back and taking the next step to buy. With the global reach and the ease of connecting through technology, there are so many ways to increase your resonance and start to build your relationship with your customer. Just as you would build a relationship with a friend or potential girlfriend or boyfriend, you need to get to know each other better. Do you both have the same interests, do you both enjoy the same things? In other words, what do you both do that resonates with each other?

How to Resonate With Your Customers – What Does Your Tribe Want?

SPIRITUAL BUSINESS TIP #22

As a business owner, your job is to make it easy for customer to get to know you.

LISA What does it mean to *resonate*? You often resonate with people who have gone through the same life experiences as you did or with people who seem to match your own personality. Perhaps they seem to understand you well, or they have solutions to the exact problems you are trying to solve. Maybe they see the world the same way you do. You feel understood in a deep way with people you resonate with.

Sometimes you feel deeply connected with them, as if they understand you or what you're going through. Often you resonate with people you feel are like you but they have accomplished, done, or learned something that you want or need.

By sharing who you are and by talking about your work you provide an opportunity for your potential customer to resonate with you. Think about why you resonate with certain people, even if they are people you don't know personally, like a teacher, author, or perhaps a TV personality. They may speak "your language" or make you feel as if they are down to earth, re-latable , or have sound views.. Keep this in mind when you want to resonate with people.

Let's break down ways you can share yourself and your work in your spiritual business so people can resonate with you.

SHARING A LIFE SITUATION – Your life situation, while unique, will have elements in it that others will relate to. For example, you may have healed yourself from a chronic problem such as an allergy to wheat and oth-ers are looking to do the same. You may have had health issues that Western medicine couldn't solve, but you found a homeopathic solution that worked like a charm. Or you found a spiritual approach that helped you have more happiness and contentment in your life.

SOLVING A PROBLEM – You solved a problem for yourself or others. For example, for my business, I wanted to become more intuitive and have control over my intuition. Every teacher, book or class I took on intuition and psychic development did not show the exact steps and process they went through to become highly intuitive along with control and reliability. Information was vague and nebulous, saying to "go into your heart" or "you'll know it when it happens to you."

Through research, experimenting, and learning I developed my own intuition from scratch. I discovered the exact steps and process to hone intuition skills, and the exercises that helped me to become psychic. With my background in psychophysiology, I studied the psychobiology and metaphysical energy mechanisms behind intuition and combined that knowledge to make it work.

I can now share this knowledge with others to help them to make their intuition strong and controllable as I did without their having to do all the research and take dozens of classes. Think about what problem does your business solve that is a problem your customer also wants to solve for themselves.

BEING DOWN TO EARTH AND RELATABLE – People relate to people they feel comfortable with. If you present yourself and your business as big and distant, it's harder to relate to. Coming from the corporate and science world, my writing and speaking was often in the third person. I used big words and phrases that made me sound scholarly or knowledgeable. My writing was hard to personally relate to. I changed my tone and the words to be more conversational.

What forced me to do this was my radio show. I wrote out the script for every show, and it had to sound as if I were speaking naturally. This required me to write as if I were talking to someone. That changed my writing completely! It also made my radio shows much more interesting to listen to because it sounded as if I were talking to you alone. Now I like to read and hear myself!

BE ORDINARY AND HAVE AN EXTRAORDINARY EXPERIENCE THAT TRANSFORMED YOU – A common reason why people start spiritual businesses is because they had a spiritually transformative experience that changed their lives. A spiritually transformative experience may be as simple as an epiphany during meditation or it may be a near-death experience.

People can resonate with those who have had an extraordinary experience because they feel, "if it can happen to normal everyday people, it can happen to me, too, or anyone else." People believe in you when they can relate to you and your experience.

BEING YOU! – Give away samples of what you do or sell. The best way for people to resonate with you is to experience a sample of your services or try out your product for free. Most people want to try before they buy, or at least get a better understanding of what it is they are buying.

Wouldn't you like to take a new car for a test drive before you purchase it? It gives potential customers a way to see if they like what you have to offer and, more important, if they resonate with you and/or your product.

Using the Internet to reach more people in a compelling way makes it easier to learn about you, your services or your product. When they learn more about you, the more they can resonate with you. The more they can experience you easily, such as through the Internet, the more strongly they can resonate with you.

Because so many people are connected to the Internet you can share lots of information in myriad ways more easily and inexpensively. Much of what we talked about so far can be easily and effectively implemented on the Internet.

You would be surprised at how many spiritual business entrepreneurs do not give people an easy way to find information about their businesses! We are going to show you some of those easy ways so you can build your relationship with your future customers.

CINDY   This is not a contradiction to my advice to not give your sessions for free. Free or discounted introductory services is a specific technique for resonating. Although, it is important to specify the value of what the customer is receiving as well as limit the amount of free or discounted services.

Ways to Reach Out and Touch People

LISA   Now that you have the elements of what helps people resonate with you, how do you get it out there and touch people? You have your personal stories, your examples of how you overcame obstacles, how you honed your skills turning problems into solutions, and you have the authenticity of being you. How do people experience all of these in order to resonate with you?

There are several different modes that you can use to get yourself "out there" and share yourself with others. We'll go over each mode and then specifically how you use these modes via in-person methods or using technology through social media, Internet marketing, and online resources.

VIDEO – Record a video of yourself. From recording a video on your cell phone to capturing video and recording yourself on your laptop, making videos is now easier than ever. High-quality videos can be recorded with an iPhone. While many of you may be shy about being recorded on video, it has the best impact when sharing who you are and what you do in order to resonate with other people.

If you think about your own preferences, wouldn't you much rather relate to someone you can see and hear, than someone you read about or just listen to? You can video-record your story, your problem solution, or share information about your products and services.

Videos don't need to be fancy, and when you are starting out you can use whatever recording device you have available. The key ingredients in video are sound and lighting. Sound is most important so make sure your audio is clear and easily understandable, which is not what you would expect in video, and pay attention to the lighting. You want to have good lighting so you can be seen easily.

CINDY Videos need to be short. Most people will tune out after a minute or two unless they have already resonated with you and like your content. I recommend producing your introduction videos to be one minute at the most. If you have recorded a class, then break the video into short segments rather than putting the whole class online.

SPIRITUAL BUSINESS TIP #23

Creating an audio recording of your story is a great way for people to resonate with you.

LISA AUDIO – Create an audio recording of you speaking. An audio recording about you and your story, particularly when you are telling it, is a dynamic way for people to resonate with you. A popular way to use audio to get your message out there is Internet radio. Lots of programing services online will let you create your own radio show for free. You just need a computer and a microphone, and away you go to record your show. For example, an online Internet radio service called Blogtalkradio.com does not require much fancy equipment, just your phone and a computer with an Internet connection.

WRITING – Write about your experiences, your story and your business. You can write articles for magazines, both online and in print. You can write your own blog or write on your website. You can write a book and self-publish it. People still do read books!

I write for several online magazines fairly regularly. Write consistently and frequently for one or two online magazines that fits your target market.

SPEAKING – One of the best ways to get exposure is public speaking. Again, this may be similar to video for many people in that you may be shy about being in front of a crowd. You can join a Toastmasters group – where people learn how to do public speaking – to help you gain your confidence and learn about public speaking.

If you are not afraid of speaking and are looking for opportunities to speak, the first places to look are local health and wellness fairs. Often you can pay to speak at these events. You can also speak at holistic centers giving a mini-class or lecture.

DOING – Giving people a chance to experience your services or products is the best way to truly give them an opportunity to resonate with what you do. You can offer mini samples for free, or at a very reduced price in the form of a special offer.

THE KEY TO CONSTANT BUSINESS FLOW – THE SALES FUNNEL

LISA How does resonating with your customer help you? Where is it going and how does resonating get a customer to purchase? Potential customers who resonate with us are "falling through the sales funnel."

That is the process by which potential customers get to know you: from first being attracted, to getting to know about you, your services and products, and then wanting to purchase them.

The metaphor uses the funnel shape because the concept is that many potential customers have to be exposed to you, ie., know who you are, what you're offering, and how to reach you, in order to ultimately get a few to buy.

ATTRACT
Spark new customer
interest

RESONATE
Engage "self-selected"
customers

SYNERGIZE
Reward loyal
customers

The New Sales Funnel.

Let's talk about what a "sales funnel" is. Traditionally, a sales funnel was the process of making a sale by convincing someone to buy. In this process people who were in your target market became potential "leads," and if they were interested in you or your business they became "prospects." As they became more comfortable learning more about you and your business, they became "qualified prospects." When they bought your services, they became "customers."

This older process was composed of sales steps, which often made people run, because they felt like they were being being given a hard-sell. That being said, this process still works, and many aspects of it are valuable — after all, people still want to buy services and products. The question is how do you convince people to buy what you're selling without the hard-sell?

If you think about the ways you yourself have become a loyal customer you may understand. You started out getting to know a business first and eventually became an avid buyer of its products — that is, you were "falling through the sales funnel."

For example, say there is a new ice-cream store in town and they are giving away free samples as you walk by. You try a taste sampler and to your delight it is delicious and may be the best ice cream you've had in a long time, certainly better than what you can find in the grocery store. So you decide to buy a pint and bring it home to your family. Well, your family loves it, and now they all want more, so you bring the kids and your spouse on your next trip to the new store to buy a gallon of the same flavor, plus you all have cones of some other flavors that sound good.

Everyone is really enjoying their ice cream and you pick up a few business cards to give to your friends and tell them about this amazing ice cream. On your next trip, with a girlfriend, you find out that they also make ice-cream cakes and do catering for children's birthday parties.

You make a mental note and the next time your child has a birthday party you use the store to cater it. Then, whenever you want to buy ice cream, there is only one place you'd ever go, this place. That is how you have become a loyal customer or have "fallen" through their "sales funnel."

More recently, the sales funnel has evolved to become a metaphor for either the process that someone goes through as he or she becomes a loyal customer, or the process that a person goes through from being introduced to a product until ultimately purchasing that product.

They may be introduced by obtaining your product or service for free or the introduction is through their purchasing a lower cost product or service. Many people may become exposed to you, but the odds are that only a few will eventually purchase from you. It's not you; it's just a matter of human likes and/or the ability to purchase, no one thing can be liked by everyone and not everyone who wants to purchase can or is able to purchase at that moment.

Simply put, you need to reach a large number of people to get a few to buy, and a large number of your first time buyers will produce a smaller number of loyal customers who are going to love what you do and sell, keep buying more, and refer you to friends. Those who are not interested going through your funnel fall out of it, ie., don't purchase or don't come back, and that is often referred to as a leaky funnel. Leaky funnels are okay, the key is to get enough people into your funnel so you can have a larger number who stick around and buy, or buy more.

The New Sales Funnel – Easier, Faster, More Convincing

SPIRITUAL BUSINESS TIP #24

The new sales funnel allows your potential customer to experience your services or products free or low cost.

LISA The new funnel is similar to the old sales funnel, only instead of the old funnel model of selling, selling, selling, the new sales funnel is allowing your potential customer to experience your services or products. Experiencing is much more powerful than trying to convince someone how good your service or product is.

In the new approach you are interacting, engaging, and allowing your potential customer to be involved with and experience your business first hand. You do this by giving the prospective customer valuable content or product over a longer period of time rather than just a one-off sample.

In the new model you are constantly giving potential customers more value as they move through the funnel. They know your product or service and strongly resonate with you. Those who are not interested fall out of the funnel, so those who stick around are what are known as "self-selecting." They continue to follow you and engage because they are interested.

Now you are left with a highly engaged, highly interested, and ready-to-buy set of people. These customers are more ready to purchase a higher priced item because they have had more experience and resonate more strongly with your business than a customer who had one small brief sample of it.

This set of highly engaged and extremely interested people should now be on your email list, so you can now engage with directly and offer your services or products to them. This is the power of the updated approach.

It is well known that a customer who has already bought from you is much more likely to buy again. By using the new funnel you can get quite a few people to experience engaging with you and your service or product without having to get over the huge hump of spending money first. It is more likely that they will become "customers" before they are customers.

Here are some examples of how you can get people to be engaged with you in your new funnel. If you are an intuitive reader you can give a few 15-minute readings away for free or for a special low rate. Make sure that you let people know that this low rate is for a limited time only.

I give listeners of our radio show free one-question angel readings on the air. An herbalist can give away small samples of his or her herbal remedies. You can record a video of your talk if you are a speaker or teacher, and then post it online. You can give some sample classes at a holistic center or other venue.

RESONATE - ONLINE WITH
INTERNET MARKETING

Leveraging the Power of Technology - Email Marketing, Blogs, Video, Podcasts and Others

SPIRITUAL BUSINESS TIP #25

Technology has allowed the entrepreneur to conduct business like the big companies.

LISA Technology allows us to connect with customers by building a relationship with them in a way that traditional print media cannot.

You can build your relationship with others more easily, and faster, with more depth and meaning. You can tap into problems people might have and provide solutions for them merely by posting on social media or contacting them in email, and get an immediate response.

By listening and responding to people's wants and needs you can build your business and its services or products. When you can touch others through your thoughts and concerns, your connection with them builds and they feel more comfortable working with you. This is how the world has changed for people like you and me who want to start our own business from scratch.

CINDY Yes, the Internet is the best way to give your prospective customers a way to get to know you. Over the years I have done more and more successful marketing on the Internet. When I first started, all my marketing was done through the mail and newspaper ads. I stopped doing newspaper ads (unless I put an ad in a New Age magazine) because it had become a waste of money.

I spent most of my budget at the post office and on printing costs. Before having a blog, I spent a fortune mailing out a newsletter. Boy, am I glad the Internet arrived! In the past I had to spend a lot more time getting my name out with mailings of brochures and notifications of classes. Now I can put a digital press kit on my website, a bio page, and a calendar that lists my book signings, classes, and psychic fairs.

Email Lists

LISA *The* most important thing you can do for your business survival is to keep an email list. The most powerful way to build your business and gain more customers is through building your email list. This goes for all businesses whether you are a brick-and-mortar shop, a solo entrepreneur, or a growing small business. It's not just a list of customer names nor is it a list of their home addresses. It is specifically a list of the email addresses and, at most, a first and last name, of people who are interested in your business.

SPIRITUAL BUSINESS TIP #26

THE most important thing you can do for your business survival is to keep an email list.

LISA If you want to get more sign-ups on your email list don't ask for too much information. People are generally reluctant to give away more than just their email address and perhaps their name. Email has become the most indispensible way to communicate for almost everyone and is the most effective way to stay connected to potential customers.

Back when I was studying in college we all had email. This was before the general population had email and when I graduated, I felt isolated and hamstrung without a quick easy way to communicate with my friends and colleagues.

I was jealous of those who had access to email. Most people can now identify with this. There are so many of us who grab our smart phones to check our email the moment we get out of bed! That means if you have an email list of potential customers who are interested in what you have to offer, your email will reach them before they ever look at their snail mail.

When you build your email list properly, you will have a powerful way to reach people who are already "self-selected" to resonate with you. The key thing is building your list the right way.

SPIRITUAL BUSINESS TIP #27

The best place to put an email opt-in box is on the upper right-hand corner of your homepage.

LISA The right way to build your list is to ask those people *who are interested* in your business to sign up to receive your newsletters and emails. You can do this most easily through what is known as an "opt-in" form on your website where people can sign up by entering their name and email address. The *best* place to put this opt-in form is in the upper right-hand corner of your home page on your website where it will not be missed.

By allowing people to choose to receive your email, they have been "self-selected" to find out more about you and receive your newsletters. They are already "qualified" as someone who feels they resonate with you. That's a great place to be, because you now are talking to someone who wants to know more about you and your business. Of course, you need to know what to put in your emails so people open them. We'll go over that next.

A CAVEAT: Never buy an email list. If you buy a list, you don't know where the email addresses came from, and emailing people who did not specifically ask to be on your list is illegal. Most of us know what spam is and we all hate it. Spam is unsolicited email and is illegal to send out. You don't want to get in trouble for sending out spam.

Picking up business cards at events, or collecting email addresses you find on the Internet and then emailing those people is also considered unsolicited email — and spam. It doesn't matter what kind of email you send; if the person you are sending it to did not ask to be on your list, it is spam.

The anti-spam laws require that you include a physical address for your business at the bottom of the your email and a way for the addressee to unsubscribe. If you don't want to use your actual home address, you can purchase a P.O. Box from your local post office and use that. The cost of a P.O. Box is minimal, and in my mind, worth it.

The reason why email lists are so powerful is because you can now reach people more directly and more frequently for very low cost. In addition, a big advantage with today's technology is that you can get insight into who is actually opening your emails, know whether they are being read by seeing if the recipient is clicking through on the links in them and find out where the readers are from and how often they open your email.

For example, I know that most of the people who open my emails are within the tri-state area of New York, New Jersey and Connecticut. That is probably because I have focused doing business in-person in these areas. Roughly 87% of the emails that are opened are from people in the United States, the rest are from around the world. I have about a 30% open rate while the industry average is 18%.

I also know how many people clicked on a link in the emails I've sent. This is very useful because it shows which things people seem to be interested in. I can also send emails to a group within my list and no one else. For example, I can send an email only to the people who are interested in my intuition/psychic development group who meet with me locally.

The best way to use email to resonate with your customers or potential customer is to send them content that they value. What does that mean? You can send tips or information that is relevant to what you do. For example, I send out monthly intuition tips and ways that people can improve their intuition on their own.

I try to make my emails interesting and entertaining as well as look appealing. I enjoy creating my emails, even though they do tend to take some time to write. One of the things I love about making them is I get to exercise the right side of my brain, which is the intuitive side, by using my visual creativity.

I love to pick graphics and pictures for my newsletters. I have had quite a few people say they love to read my newsletters and that they are so beautiful to look at. You don't have to go this far in your newsletters, and there is a philosophy out there that says a plain text email works better than a fancier one. The theory is that people like to read emails from their friends and not from a big company with fancy headers and advertising. But bottom line is fancy or not, email communication works.

SPIRITUAL BUSINESS TIP #28
People don't want to get an email that is just full of advertising.

LISA The important thing is to have good content, which is useful and interesting to your readers. As an angel reader, an email that people would want to read can be to send angel prayers for different situations. You can send those out in an email once a month. Or you may want to send out emails that answer frequently asked questions you hear from your customers.

That is the best kind of email to send because not only are you giving great content but also it's the kind of content that people want because they've asked for it.

CINDY I have found the same thing as Lisa, that my "open" rates are greatly increased when my emails contain more content than marketing. That said, you can of course put some marketing or your schedule of events toward the end of your email. Just remember, content is primary, marketing is secondary.

Email Marketing

The most powerful way to build your business is by building your email list.

LISA What is email marketing? Email marketing is directly marketing to your potential customers through email in the form of newsletters, sales letters, or simply conversational letters. You don't need a special service to do email marketing, though it would be "best practice" to use an email marketing service provider because they are equipped to handle a large volume of email and also help you comply with anti-spam laws.

Email marketing is one of the most effective and easy ways to stay in touch with your customers and your potential customers. Email to opt-in lists can generally yield higher results than direct mail, that is, snail mail, at a lower cost.

Once you begin to build your email list of customers, you will need a place to put that list so it is easy to maintain, edit, and add to. Email marketing service providers, such as Constant Contact, MailChimp, Aweber and iContact, will give you forms that you can put on your website so people can sign up for your list easily. They will store those email addresses, and give you a way to create beautiful email using professional-looking templates and then send those emails out for you.

The advantages to using an email marketing service provider are that they do not have restrictions on how many emails they can send at once, their templates have information in them to comply with anti-spam laws, and they test and work with Internet Service Providers (ISPs) to help make sure emails are delivered. Creating an email through these services is often like using a word processor. Some of them provide images that you can use without worrying about copyright violations. In addition, many also provide ways to embed a link or a form to connect to your website so people can sign up directly. In this way, people can sign up for your list while you are asleep!

Email is a great way to communicate valuable information that is related to your services and products. You can share information such as tips and related uses or benefits of your products. You can provide information about your services and products and how to reach you in other ways when you are online or off-line.

People don't want to get email that is full of advertising. If your email is purely advertising, people are most likely going to unsubscribe from your list. You may want to start paying attention to the kinds of email you get every day in your inbox and take note of the emails you like to read and the ones you just delete. You can use those emails as a model for what you may want, and not want, to send out to your customers.

Using an Email Service Provider saves time and aggravation.

CINDY The thing I like about using an email management service provider is that it often will handle those pesky 'unsubscribes' for you. This is a huge timesaver, and you're less likely to annoy people with more emails after they have unsubscribed. Another point to think about with emails is frequency.

When I ask for someone's email address, I tell him or her that I don't email frequently because I myself don't like to get a lot of mail from businesses. Then you need to be honest on the follow-up. Emailing too much, and emailing only sales stuff is the fastest way to get someone to unsubscribe from your list. I also let people know they can simply unsubscribe at the bottom of the email if they don't want the information anymore.

This is a requirement of the Can-Spam Act (*Controlling the Assault of Non-Solicited Pornography And Marketing Act of 2003*). The sender must include a way to unsubscribe from email. To make sure your emails are compliant, search Anti-Spam Act to get the most recent requirements.

If you email too often, you'll find that people delete your mail. Remember, it is better to have a smaller list than a big one in which the client automatically sends your email to the trash. If someone is emailing me every week, I stop reading the emails. If they send more than that, I unsubscribe.

Another advantage of email services is that you can separate your list into groups based on their interest. If you are doing an event like a holistic fair in a small town in Upstate New York, you don't want to send an email about it to someone in Arizona, but if you are teaching a weekend workshop in Arizona, then by all means, include Arizona! This is why it's important to know what state the person is from, or a zip code.

Many of these programs allow you to use the first name of the email recipient in the text of the email. I find this is a great feature — it makes the person feel like you took the time to send him or her an email personally and will attract more attention.

When using email, it is important to:

- Send quality content like tips or other valuable information, along with your marketing.
- Send emails on a reasonable time schedule, not too frequently. Use an email marketing service.
- Make your email easy to read, with graphics if possible.
- Personalize your email to fit the client's interest.

LISA One of the key components in email marketing is to get as many people as you can who are attracted to your business <u>on</u> your email list.

If they are not on your email list, then you cannot build your relationship with them and communicate consistently. This is why your email list is the most important part of growing your business. It is a key part of Internet marketing and a major part of the Resonate stage of marketing. When you automate growing your email list through technology, you are going to catapult your business to the next level more quickly.

You do not need a large list to be effective in gaining customers. If you're just starting out, your list is going to be small. It may start with a few customers and some of your family and friends. Don't discount the value of your family or friends on your list. People on your list don't necessarily have to be customers; they can also be your advocates. When they know what it is you do and are up-to-date with your services or events they can spread the word for you.

You don't need to be fancy in the beginning and feel you need to integrate your email marketing system right away. Just start with an opt-in box on your website. Then grow from there, which is what I did. It took me a while to have lots of automation in place. Remember, whatever promotional material you have, wherever you perform your services, sell your products, hold a workshop or speaking engagement, get people to sign up for your email list. These are perfect places and opportunities to find people who will want to sign up for your list.

The easiest way you get people to sign up for your list is to have an email opt-in box on your webpage. It is also important that you do not ask for too much information in your opt-in box. Most people are reluctant to give too much of their private information. Again, a name and email address is enough. You can shorten it even more by just asking for a first name and email address. This is probably the minimum that you should ask for since just having an email address prevents you from personalizing your emails and addressing them to a name. But, don't be too greedy in asking for information.

Remember, most people are reluctant to give out too much information when asked for their email address, even if they are getting a free gift in return. You will get more sign-ups for your list by asking for less information. The great thing about email marketing technology is that you don't need to ask people what state they are from; it will show up in the email system when they open your email. This is how the email marketing program can target locations.

CINDY Remember, never add a person's email unless you get permission. It might seem tempting to take emails from ads and websites, but those are the people who will report you for spam since they didn't ask to be on your list. *Too many spam reports and you'll get blacklisted.*

SPIRITUAL BUSINESS TIP #31
It is better to have a smaller list than a big one where the client just deletes your email.

LISA In my opinion one of the rudest things to do is pick up other people's business cards at a public event, and then, without their knowledge, add their email addresses to your list. I've had this happen many times to me and it is really irritating aside from violating Anti-Spam laws.

CINDY There are many accepted ways to build your email list. A few ways to increase your email list are to:

- Hand out a sign-up sheet when you do events and talks, asking for name and email address.
- Always keep a little pad with you or use a notes app on your phone to take down people's email when you are networking.
- Ask for contact information anytime you meet with a new client, which should include email.

Online Writing – Blogs and Online Magazines

LISA Writing can be a great way to resonate with other people. Your writing doesn't need to be perfect and you don't need to be a novelist or a professional writer. Some of the things that you can write about are:

- What your business is about
- Your philosophy on your business
- Your tips for living well
- A preview of things you do in your business
- The benefits of your business
- What you have learned through practicing your business.

For example, let's say that you are a massage therapist; you could write about different kinds of massage techniques and what they're good for. In your business, if you specialize in a particular modality you can write about that. For example if you're an energy healer, and you specialize in Reiki, you can write about what Reiki is and how it helps people.

You can put your writing in a blog. A blog is like an online diary or list of articles. It is a website that lists out diary or article entries. These entries are listed in date order or you can categorize them into groups.

SPIRITUAL BUSINESS TIP #32
A blog or article should be between 400 and 1000 words.

The wonderful thing about blogs is that there are places online that you can create one for free. Currently, the most popular blogging tool is WordPress. com, where you can set up your own blog free. With a little online research, you can find multiple blog sites.

Another free blogging tool is Blogger.com, owned by Google, which offers a great advantage because Google will search any blogs that are posted here very well. I have a Bogger.com blog for my psychic development tips and it gets quite a bit of traffic.

Once you have a blog, you can write the entries on anything you wish. You can then give people the address to your blog and they can go and see what you've written. You can send your blog link to people on your email list when you have a new post and include the link in your monthly emails as well. You can also print business cards or postcards with the address to your blog to increase traffic.

Another way you can get your writing seen is to write for an online magazine. Online magazines have become very popular and there are quite a few organizations that now publish magazines online. Even the print magazines are offering online versions. Pick a magazine that has subscribers in your target market.

I have been writing for OmTimes Magazine for the past three years. Their target market is the same as mine so it reaches many potential customers who could be interested in what I do. Many of these magazines have editors who screen article submissions from people who submit them. They often have requirements as to how long the article needs to be and what the article should be written about.

You should review the online magazine first to see if your article topics and your style of writing fit with what they already publish. Make sure your writing has been proofread and that you are submitting good quality work. Also look at the terms and conditions to see what they allow you to do with the article you submit if they were to publish it.

Some magazines will not allow you to publish the same article in other places. Some magazines will say that you can publish the article on your website but not in other publications. These magazines will also tell you the minimum and maximum length for the article they will accept.

Online magazines have great statistics available on their subscriber numbers, how many people are looking at their pages and their articles as well as how long people stay on a particular page. Digital analytics can break down demographics of visitors to a site or a webpage and even know which pages visitors came from to get to a particular article.

Google Analytics provides this information as well as other companies that specialize in this service. These magazines know what types of consumer are reading their articles. If you read their advertising media package, they often list these statistics. This can help you identify which online magazines have an audience that matches your target market. Just look for information about advertising on their site.

A big advantage to writing an article for an online magazine is that it can be easily shared through social media. Those "shares" or "likes" are often listed on the page of the article itself. That can help you to know which types of articles are read most in a particular online magazine. You can then target writing those kinds of articles for that magazine.

Of course, you can also write articles for your newsletter. I highly recommend that you do write some sort of article that gives good content and value to your newsletter readers. This is a good way to help people resonate with you. Again, you don't need to write a book, as your article should be between 400 to 1000 words. Be sure to check with the publications you're writing for on their word minimums and maximums.

Video & Vlogs

LISA Creating videos of yourself speaking and demonstrating about your business, or what you do, is a very powerful tool to create resonance with propective clients. Many of you may be camera-shy. I was very camera-shy in the beginning. People relate to what they see and hear better than to what they read.

Humans are visual creatures and they like to see the person that they are trying to get to know; they *want* to see your video. There are a lot of ways that you can record and get your videos out there. Most smart phones have a way to record a video and many computers have a camera built right in.

Your video does not have to be super high-definition quality, but you should pay attention to lighting and how the camera is positioned in front of you. You don't want to be looking down into the camera or up into the camera. You should be looking straight at it.

Also, make sure that you are lit from the front. If your lighting is behind you, you will be backlit, creating shadows on your face.

Many camcorders, smartphones, tablets, and laptops will record a video and then upload it to social networking sites fairly easily. You can learn about the online tools to publish videos in the help or support section of their websites or search online. There are amazing "how to" videos online for almost anything you will need.

Today, most people use Google as a search engine tool for finding things on the Internet. Many people don't realize that currently YouTube search is one of the biggest and most widely used search engines aside from Google. That may be in part because Google owns it.

YouTube is just as frequently used as a search engine and can help you be known to potential customers. Just to show you the power of YouTube, here is an example of how putting a video on YouTube can bring traffic to your website and generate potential customers.

I posted on YouTube a video recording of my talk on "The 10 Key Secrets to Intuition." I posted it on a whim, because the video was meant to be a way for me to see how I could improve my public speaking style. I posted the video on YouTube not thinking much about it with a link to my website. The video has reached over 18,000 views. What amazed me was that some people from Canada and California discovered the video and after watching, they were motivated to travel to New York for my class.

If you enjoy creating videos you may want to start a Vlog, which is a video blog. You can do this very easily on YouTube by creating your own YouTube "channel," which is a page where all your videos are posted. People can then subscribe to your YouTube channel (vlog) and be notified of when you post updates. Video is very powerful in that it can convey your message, provide potential customers with tons of information and allow them to resonate with you.

It is much easier to resonate with someone you can see and hear, than just hear or perhaps read about.

Internet Radio and Audio Podcasts

LISA Audio can still be a great way to resonate with people because they like to listen to audio broadcasts or podcasts while they are doing other things. For example many people listen to audio recordings or live audio when they are on their way to work or going for a walk.

Recorded audio is really powerful because people can listen anytime. You can record a mini lesson, a lecture, a meditation or you can record anything that you have written.

Some of the ways you can use technology to get your audio out to other people is to have an Internet radio show. These radio shows are broadcast live just like a radio show you listen to over traditional radio. The only difference is that they are on the Internet and people listen through their computer or dial-in over the phone.

I have an Internet radio talk show called *Between Heaven and Earth*, and since 2008 we've broadcast once a month. We have thousands of listeners per show and most of the people that listen actually listen to the archives. I've had people come to me and say they've been listening to us for years. Creating a radio show is very easy to do and is becoming a very popular way to resonate with potential customers. Cindy can talk more about her experiences with radio as she had a show with her husband.

CINDY Dave and I created an Internet radio show called *Spiritual Simplicity*. At the time, we didn't have Lisa's marketing skills and Internet radio was not quite established. We paid for our radio time and our show was costly to put on, without giving us much immediate return. So you might wonder whether it was worth it?.

I didn't get one reading out of the shows we put on, yet there were still many benefits. Not everything is about how many clients you get from what you are offering. We made a lot of connections that saw fruition down the road when we published our first book, and, if we had chosen, we could have marketed the recordings from our show. Nowadays, as Lisa mentioned, you can get Internet radio time for low cost or free.

The Key to Online Success – Communicate Consistently and Frequently!

SPIRITUAL BUSINESS TIP #33

To resonate with your potential customers, the most important thing is consistency. Send out your newsletter or email regularly.

LISA If you're going to resonate with your potential customers the most important thing is consistency. That means you should be putting out a email or newsletter on a periodic basis. I try to send out a newsletter once a month; some suggest that you send something out once a week.

I try to balance it out so I am not inundating anyone's inbox with emails. The great thing about Internet Marketing is that it works at all levels of the sales funnel all the time. You're able to attract, resonate, and as you will see, synergize with your customers with Internet marketing.

Many people find that social media is a little burdensome to consistently keep up with, asking if they could get someone else to do the posting to their social media accounts. I suggest that you do not have someone else do your social media posting because you are trying to resonate with your customers and when you put your own personal touch into your posts people will know that it's you.

If you are doing a blog post, short video or radio show, it is important that you produce and post them consistently and periodically. You should aim for at least once a month. If it is too much to do all of these things, just pick one and be consistent with that. Start with your email list and send them good content.

CINDY I agree with Lisa about doing your own posting to social media. The personal touch is so important and one of the main reasons, I think, that social networking is so popular. Yet I know a very successful and busy spiritual teacher who has someone else post "wisdom snippets" from his published book regularly and then he posts more personal messages when he has time. It is a good mix of content and personalization.

Which Do I Do First? Where Do I Start?

SPIRITUAL BUSINESS TIP #34

If you're wondering what to start with first, Facebook is better than Twitter.

LISA If you're wondering what to start with first, I suggest an email list. Email newsletters are more powerful than social media like Facebook or Twitter. Even if you are just starting out and have no list, you can begin to create one with your friends and family who are willing to be on your list, then continue to add to it.

The people on your list are self-selected and interested in finding out more about you. The problem with most social media is that not everyone will see your posts because a post has a limited life span. If you are trying to decide which is the best social media platform to work with, Facebook is better than Twitter. If you would like to write an article, blogs are good for long-term content sharing because the blog can stay online forever.

Writing for an online magazine is better than a blog because magazines tend to have a larger audience than what you can generate for your blog. That being said, a blog still has value so, if you can, write for both. I've written blog posts years ago that people still read and then sign up for my newsletter.

Again video is better than audio as video tends to work best for relationship building. But you should start with what you're comfortable with! Do not try to do everything at once. All of these things take time and it is important that you take the time to do whatever you do well and consistently.

RESONATE - IN-PERSON – LOCAL PLACES TO CONNECT

Places to Connect

Library

CINDY Giving free talks are a chance to educate and give back to your community. Libraries are the perfect place to educate prospective clients on what your specific modality is and what benefits it offers, although usually they don't allow you to charge admission. Your talk should not be one big marketing push. It is important to offer real and valuable information, while taking only a little of the time to market your services.

With that said, make sure to pass around a sign-in sheet for email contact information, hand out brochures and flyers on upcoming events, and give away some sort of discount coupon for the first time they try your services or products.

Chamber of Commerce

CINDY I belong to my local Skaneateles Chamber of Commerce, and I have found them supportive and very active in the community. We live in a lakeside town that is a favorite for tourists, and the chamber does a lot to connect both local and non-local people with their merchants. I am allowed to put my brochure in their office and I am on the Chamber's website.

The Chamber offers after-work get-togethers where you can meet other local merchants to network and also offers opportunities to advertise during local events. Not all the advertising has worked for me, but I have found that some opportunities, like being a part of a larger Chamber event in a larger city near me, worked out really well.

The yearly Chamber membership varies from place to place, but you can get a lot of networking out of membership. I recommend that you speak to your local Chamber representative and get a feel of what your Chamber can offer.

Psychic Fairs, New Age Expos, and Health Fairs

CINDY Psychic Fairs, Expos, and other holistic events are a great way to network with other practitioners while letting prospective clients learn about you. Depending on the event, spaces are often filled with Reiki practitioners, chair massage, chiropractors, psychics, and vendors of all sorts.

Fairs and Expos can be expensive and, without a professional presentation, you may find yourself sitting all day instead of working and networking. Often a vendor booth is less expensive than a practitioner booth. If you are an information-only vendor, then sometimes you can get a smaller booth and lower your costs as well. Before you sign up for a fair, visit a few of them. Look to see what kind of signs and displays the busier practitioners and vendors have. All too often I see a new psychic or other practitioner who has paid big bucks for a booth arrive with a handmade sign, put nothing on her front table other than a cloth, and then sit through the whole fair wearing a frown, arms crossed, and wondering why no one wants to talk to her.

Don't waste your money on an event until you have done your research and are ready to show up with a strong, confident presentation.

You may want to market to your existing clientele that you will be at the event by sending emails or postcards. I prefer doing both. I send a postcard to those for whom I only have snail mail addresses and emails to everyone on my list. I put the name of the event, the dates, times, and what I will be doing there.

If I am reading and have a lecture, I put the lecture time, but often I won't know my lecture time until right before the show and I mail out postcards about three weeks prior. I send the emails out twice, first about three weeks prior and then just a few days before the event. You can also create an event on social networking and post announcements that you will be attending.

I usually offer $5 off if clients pre-book an appointment. Also offer discounts to your social networking friends! How you pre-market depends on what type of event you are going to and what services, if any, you are offering.

A professional booth sign and printed price sign are a must. Many of your local office supply stores or online printing services make signs very reasonably priced. Most of these have pre-designed signs where you just pop in your information. Avoid common themes. Yes, they are pretty but you and three other vendors will all have the same sign. Look for a theme that speaks to your energy and your business specialty.

If you feel inspired, you can also create your own design. You can print price signs and flyers on your own computer. Make sure your price sign is easy to read with large print because most people don't come right up to the table. I have used digital picture frames for my price sign because a changing screen attracts attention. You won't be able to nail or tape any signs to the wall, so invest in sign stands.

After you have visited a few shows, you will know what type of booth tables you liked and which you didn't. Your table should reflect your energy. You don't want it too sparse, but avoid it being so crowded that there is too much to look at. Pay attention to color and color-coordinate your booth. You might want to match the color of the tablecloth to your back curtain or your outfit.

I use the same cloth for my front table as for my reading table. A must is the chocolate dish in order to attract people to your table. Put out the good stuff! People rarely will run to your booth for a Tootsie Roll or starburst mint! You will get a few candy trollers, but one sideways look will stop them from coming by for their fifth helping. If you leave your table, take in the candy dish, or there will be none left when you get back!

A contest bowl, where you give away something to those that sign up, is a swell addition to your table and a way to get names and emails/snail mail, to send information to after the show. I offer a 15-minute phone reading or a copy of my most recent book as a contest prize. I ask for the person's snail mail and email so that I can send a letter with my brochure right away and then emails afterward.

The entries that do not win get a letter saying they didn't win as well as my brochure and sometimes even a $5-off coupon. I also ask on the contest form if they are interested in other fairs in the area, enlightening books, and classes. That way I know which lists to put them on when I get home. No one likes junk mail, so this way I do not send everything to everyone.

The "brag book," as it is lovingly called, is a three-ring binder with information about you and your services. Mine has articles written by me and about me, information about my services, pictures, as well as my certifications. I was surprised to learn that what everyone really looks at are the pictures. I had pictures of me in front of the pyramids, at New Grange, and some other places I had traveled.

Most people ignore the impressive articles about me and go straight to the pictures. So now the majority of my brag book is filled with pictures. Yes, some are just of my vacations. The one most people look at is one my sister, Gray Tham, took of a dolphin when I was in Australia. I can't count the number of times a person said, "*I love dolphins; I'll have a reading with you!*"

The pictures in your brag book are also ice-breakers. People at shows are often afraid they will get roped in, but if we can talk about a trip they took or how much they love dolphins, they get to know me without the sales pitch. They see me as a real person, not The Psychic selling her wares!

Certain etiquette needs to be followed if you want to be invited back to a fair or expo. This is another reason to visit events beforehand so you can feel out what marketing practices are accepted and which are not. For example, where I do most of my events, it is not considered polite to stand up behind your table and you definitely should not go outside your table.

Yet I was at an event a few hours away and there if you didn't stand up behind your table, people thought you were unfriendly! With that said, it is never okay to start talking to a person before he or she has come to your table; do not offer freebies, be pushy, or talk down about someone else at the show. Over-aggressive marketing at a show is called hooking or hawking. Don't do it if you want to survive in business.

Also, watch your body language. Arms folded or reading a book is the fastest way to make people feel you are unapproachable. If you are a large or tall male, you may also need to be careful of your body language. My husband books my readings for me, and he's tall, over 6 feet. He is very careful not to stand or, if he does stand, he keeps his hands behind his back in a way that is open and not menacing. If you have a booker or another person helping out at your booth, make sure his or her appearance is open and friendly.

Tell them ahead of time that you would like them not to check their phone while in the booth and teach them about body language. The best stance, if you are standing, is with your hands clasped behind your back. Energetically it shows your heart center is open. If you are sitting or standing, avoid crossing your arms.

If the event is offering lectures, submit a proposal to do a lecture. It is good publicity and you will get your name in the program twice! You will be able to hand out your marketing information to a targeted audience. After any event, I send out a mailing. I send a thank you to anyone who had a reading with me, and a letter to all the contest entries to report contest results.

I prefer snail mailings for this purpose because I can include a brochure and maybe a coupon or bookmark for my most recent book in each letter. If I am local, I might also include a party brochure.

SPIRITUAL BUSINESS TIP #35

Lecturing and speaking at holistic events are effective ways of gaining new customers.

LISA I have done a lot of lecturing and speaking at these events and I have found it is a very effective way of gaining visibility and new customers. I used to do angel readings at public events and I would ask those who came to me to add their email address to my list. This would generate as many potential customers on my list as I could see in a day, which at most would be perhaps 20 after an entire day of doing readings. After doing a 45-minute lecture, however, I can easily collect 40 to 50 potential customers on my email list.

To obtain a lecturing or speaking spot at an event like an expo or wellness fair you will usually need to purchase an exhibit booth spot or sometimes you can just purchase an advertisement in the event brochure. Along with the purchase of a booth rental or advertisement you will often get a 40 to 55-minute speaking time during the event.

You may be able to request a day and time that works best for you, but you usually don't have much choice as to when they slot you in. Some lecture schedules will have a 5 to 10-minute break between speaking spots for transition and set-up. Sometimes they do not give you set-up time and you are expected to just walk up and speak. That can be a problem if you have materials or equipment that you use in your lecture.

The best thing is to expect a short break to no set-up time and have an assistant with you to help you organize any material you want to give out. Some places do not want you to 'sell' and require that you only give a lecture that is pure teaching or information content. You may be able to rent audiovisual equipment at an event, which will be an additional cost, or you can bring your own. I highly recommend using a microphone and speaker system if you can. It is often difficult to hear a speaker without it.

I have a small portable PA (public address) system with a wireless microphone. While it can be a little expensive, if you do a lot of speaking it is well worth it. I've even had to use it in a small setting where I gave a talk in a restaurant.

Keep your lecture short. You may think 45 minutes is a long time, but it actually is not, especially if you plan to take questions. In a smaller group setting it is important to engage your audience and encourage their participation. This helps people resonate with you since they will be more engaged. At the outset, people are hesitant to participate, but once a few do, more and more build their courage to ask a question.

The key secret to filling a room with people, that is drawing a crowd, is two things: the title of your talk and what you talk about. Put yourself in the shoes of your audience and think about what would draw you in. Titles that are specific and explain what you can specifically gain from the lecture is going to attract more people than one that is vague and "airy fairy."

For example, a lecture title that says, "More Truth Will Set You Free" doesn't really tell me much and doesn't draw my attention. One of my lectures is called, "The 10 Key Secrets to Intuition."

The first time I gave that talk the room was filled to capacity with 50 people, some of whom had to stand in the back. I would say about four people in the room came from my client list; the rest were attendees at the fair.

Bring your brochures, postcards and business cards to hand out. You should be prepared to have information on where people can purchase your products, buy your services, and attend your events. You will almost always attract people interested in learning more about you and your business when you speak.

Business cards require a special note. Please remember your business cards whenever you go to an event where you are likely to meet people. This probably means you should carry business cards all the time. A business card is a quick and convenient way to help people remember you. It's like a bookmark on the web.

At an event, people you meet may want to remember you, learn more about you later and stay in touch. Whether you are a practitioner, speaker, author or even a student at a training event, remember to bring your business cards. I've been to so many events, seminars, and even classes where I found some people I met didn't have their business cards.

During my talks I often hold a raffle for signing up on my list where the winner will get a free angel reading and then the winner announcement goes out in a follow-up email, which is often my newsletter. The raffle is also another motivator to entice people to come hear you speak.

Bookstores and Metaphysical Shops

CINDY   If you are a psychic, angel reader, channel, or even massage therapist, New Age bookstores, metaphysical shops, and boutique gift shops that cater to a holistic clientele are all excellent places to start to build your business.

You can offer classes, readings, or just get to know people by spending time there. If you teach a class or spend a day offering sessions, it is always nice to buy a little something from the store. If we don't support our local New Age shops, we'll lose them, and probably lose business ourselves.

Here are a couple of things to keep in mind when working out of a bookstore or boutique environment. The store is not responsible to keep you busy with clients — you'll need to do marketing for yourself. Social networking is a good way to start. Post an event if you are doing a class, or post where you are going to appear.

Send out emails to your list and include a link to the website of the store. Let the store know that you are promoting it as well. It is more likely they will have you back and recommend you.

With each potential client you meet, get contact information, or at least a first name and email. This is not in order to steal clients from the bookstore. Rather, it's to make sure you can let those new clients know what you are offering and when you will be back. It's important in a spiritual business to be ethical, or else you're not running a spiritual business.

This means it's OK to let them know when you will be in the area again, but you won't use the new contact if you are opening a similar store.

I use a database form that asks the client's name, address, email, and birthday. I ask for the birthday because I am also a numerologist; I then send the client a birthday card with a discount coupon! If someone doesn't want to fill out the form, don't make a big deal, but let him or her know this is how you notify people if you are doing something in their area.

If clients still don't want to give out their information, I tell them they can always check the calendar on my website to find out when I'll be in the area again. I put checkboxes on the form I use for contests so I only send the person what they are interested in. You could do this on your database form and then you will only send the client information about the parts of your business that they are interested in!

For example, I ask if they are interested in "Empowering books." If they don't check off Empowering books, then I don't send them information on my book events, only my psychic events. Granted, if I have a new book come out, I usually market to everyone at least once, but I wouldn't send to that person more than once.

Let your clients know you never give out your email list to anyone, you won't overload them with emails, and they can always opt out at the bottom of any email. And then... **don't** overload them with emails!

Usually the bookstore will ask for a cut of what you make. Don't assume that this split is the same at every store. Ask what the store expects. I learned this the hard way on a book tour. I offered a 40/60 split where I got 60 and they got 40 percent. It turned out the store usually only took 30 percent!

Also, you may find the split is different for readings than classes. Ask how much they expect from each service you are offering. Sometimes a bookstore or New Age center will simply charge a room rent. If the store takes a percentage on classes, I might ask for a cap.

For example, my friend Virginia Waldron, who runs the RoseHeart Center, asks 20% of the class tuition and in the past I have asked her if we can cap it at, say $100, if I am teaching a one-day class. She was fine with that, but now I am teaching an 8-week class and I have not asked for a cap, as I have no idea how many people I will get and she is willing to take that risk.

Whether offering readings or a class, it is important to respect the space you are in by staying on time, cleaning up after yourself by putting things back the way your find them, and supporting the space through your own marketing and purchases.

Contests and Freebies

CINDY There is no better way to create goodwill (and a good database) than by having a contest. Freebies without a contest are fine as long as they are limited and not offered often — otherwise clients will just wait until you offer freebies.

I have a contest bowl at every event. I use an old-fashioned candy jar with a sign taped to it. The sign is printed on my computer and not handwritten. I usually offer one free item, be it a 15-minute phone psychic reading or a copy of my most recent book. I then ask a neighboring exhibitor or the store clerk to pick a winner at the end of day.

I tell people they will be notified by snail mail if they win, but if email is preferred, that is fine too. I snail-mail to both the winners and the rest of the contest entrants so I can send a brochure and maybe a coupon. People tend to hold on to brochures, but not always to emails.

With all this goodwill and all the work you'll be doing to let your clients get to know you and resonate with you, you'll want them to stay with your business over the long haul. In the next chapter Lisa continues her marketing trio with how to *synergize* with your clients so that they stay with you and become long-term customers.

CHAPTER SEVEN

Growing and Maintaining Your Business – SYNERGIZE!

· · · · · · · · · · · · · · · · ·

LISA Once you establish your initial group of customers you'll want to continue to grow your business. That means you'll need to maintain and grow your relationship with them as well as continue to attract and resonate with new customers. The process of having your customers get to know you and your work, then building and maintaining a relationship with them is a way of developing "synergy" with them.

This process of synergizing is how the end of the sales funnel works. The concept is that as you connect with many people, they will "test" you out to see if they want to purchase from you. Some will resonate and go to the first step of trying out what you do, and others will move on.

Some of those who try you and your work will stay and purchase more, others will not. They are moving through an imaginary funnel. Those that "fall" all the way through will be your most loyal customers.

SPIRITUAL BUSINESS TIP #36
Building and maintaining a relationship with your customers is a way of developing "synergy" with them.

To grow your business you'll want to have as many customers as you can go through your funnel. Even those who do not purchase from you right away may still do so later, so you want to keep in touch. In addition, once you have your first customer or group of customers you'll want to keep them coming back. So how do you do this? By "synergizing" with them.

SYNERGIZE – WHAT IS IT?

LISA Synergizing is like taking your relationship with an acquaintance to the next level of being friends, and then going from good friends to perhaps close friends. Have you ever been a fan of a celebrity by watching them on

TV or in the movies, and you see them so often, you feel like you almost know them as a friend? You begin to trust the celebrity and want to keep up with what he or she is doing.

Or perhaps you always get your breakfast at the same coffee shop every day and get to know the owner behind the counter. Over time, through your small talk, you get to know a little bit about each other and you feel you are friends.

You love the products at this coffee shop and they always have your favorite type of coffee. The shop owner knows what you like to have for breakfast and when he sees you he is ready to make it for you.

Then a new coffee franchise opens up across the street, but you're reluctant to change from your favorite coffee shop because of the synergizing relationship you have with them. You're a loyal customer on many levels. You even build this synergizing connection with people you see on the way to work, say on the train platform as you see the same people take the same train every day.

You may not even talk to each other, but you begin to recognize each other and you are silently connected through a routine that you both do every day. This is the synergy working! You've become connected in a way that has lasting effects. Because of that connection you are more likely to be a loyal fan, customer, or friend!

SPIRITUAL BUSINESS TIP #37

People want to connect and stay connected. Your job is to help them want to be connected to you.

As a business owner or entrepreneur, building those close relationships with your customers is important. The good thing is we, as humans, are social creatures. It is in our biology to be social and be connected. Our social nature is what makes us powerful as a species. People want to connect and stay connected. Your job is to help them want to be connected to you. Synergizing is not only a key way to maintain your customer relationships but also important in growing your business.

How to Keep Your Customers Coming Back

LISA   One of the ways you can help people who want to be connected to you is by "staying in front of them." This means whether they see your advertising or know about your events, read your blog or hear your podcast, they are always aware of your presence. Granted this takes a bit of work and consistency but it is important!

In tracking my customers over years, and as most marketing experts will tell you, your best customers will be those who already bought from you. They are more willing to spend with you again. Keeping in front of people can be done many ways, and remember that even an event they paid to attend is a form of advertising and staying noticed.

The most cost effective, and in some cases free, way to stay in touch is through advertising, social media, or emailing your list.

SPIRITUAL BUSINESS TIP #38

Your best customers will be those who already bought from you.

I know the first question you're going to ask is how often do I need to be in front of someone? The best answer is, it depends on your schedule and how you are reaching people. If you are emailing your list, the minimum should be at least once a month.

With social media you can post at least a few times a week, if not every day. There are so many ways now that you can stay in front of your customers for very little cost. It's easy to do, and you just have to make the time to do it. You can synergize online or in-person.

❄ ❄ ❄ ❄

Synergizing is also important to growing your business. Because your existing customers are the most likely to purchase from you, it is vital that you have something for them to buy! You need to make sure that you have more products and services to offer. The best time to offer your next level of service or product is a time when your customer has just bought from you or they are just finished with using your services, in other words when they are engaged with your business..

For example, normally, when I am teaching my two-day Developing Your Intuition Level One class I will start to talk about Level Two to the students half way through the session. I then end the day promoting this next class giving the students a time-limited special price, which expires at the end of the day.

Growing your business means constantly providing more products and services that customers can buy at any stage of the relationship process. If you only focus on bringing in new customers and ignore your existing customers you will be loosing a large opportunity to take your business to the next level.

You can offer another level of service or product, or you can provide an "add-on" product that adds value to an existing service or product. This is known as an "upsell." Because a customer has bought something from you and already likes what you offer, he or she is more likely to buy more from you. Upsells can be very successful for increasing business without requiring a hard sell.

That means you need something to add on or be able to provide as the next level of product or service. Your job as a business owner is to create a few levels of products or services. The longevity of your business relies on both your ability to bring in new customers and keep your existing customers coming back for more.

That means you need to have products and services. Let's talk about how you can create upsells and different-tiered products to grow your business and create loyal happy customers.

Offer More: Products and Services

LISA Upsells can be adding on to an existing product or service you offer or it can be exposing your customer to other things they can purchase that they may not have considered.

You can also offer an upgrade to what your customer is interested in. Of course, you will need more products and services to offer as upsells, so again, part of your work is to create those. Here are some examples of "add-on" or upgrades to services.

A massage therapist may add-on using aromatic oils, providing a hot stone massage, or perhaps a moisturizing wax treatment. An energy healer who does Reiki may add-on sound healing or use crystals. I have often offered my Angel Readings with a quick energy healing. Your modified offers may also help distinguish you from other practitioners as well. If you are an intuitive reader, you may want to offer specialized readings in business, relationships, or animal communication.

In general, you can offer different levels of products or services. Breaking them out into three tiers of low, middle, and high groups may help you organize them. Your lowest tier may even include services you do for free or almost free.

Low-tier products and services are the least expensive and easiest for your new customers to purchase. This gives your customers a chance to experience your business at a lower cost, perhaps it is a shorter session or a simpler or smaller product.

Mid-tier products or services may be the mainstay which most customers buy and what you see is central to your business offering.

The high-tier products may be the advanced level services or perhaps the luxury products that have all special perks and add-ons included. Usually the higher-tiered products or services are sold at a higher price. What the customer gets for these higher tiers is more for their money. For the low tiers, don't forget to offer some free items, which can be samples, because these are also good for prospective customers and existing customers to encourage them to try and buy more.

You can take advantage of what is known as "selling at the back of the room" at your events. Say you are giving a workshop or you are giving a talk and you have engaged your audience, many of them will be interested in purchasing from you right then.

It's important to have something to offer them at that moment since most people may either forget to follow up with you later to buy, or they may not be as interested as time goes on because they may not be as excited about purchasing later.

As much as we believe we purchase through logic, most of us really buy on impulse. That's not to say that you're not happy later with your purchase, it's just that we all buy when the 'mood' strikes us. You want to be ready to capture people when they are in the "mood" to buy from you. This is usually right after your talk or workshop.

If you have many things to sell in your business you'll be ready to capture them at that time. Remember to bring your products or be ready to take appointments for your services when you are "selling from the back of the room."

CINDY Some events don't allow any sales, and in that case, it is prudent to always have a brochure or handout that lists your products and services, with a coupon or "show special" with a quick expiration date, so that the attendee is motivated to purchase before the excitement of your event wears down.

This is not implying that you are not a good speaker; it is simply human nature, as Lisa noted, to impulse-buy. Often there is not time after your event to hang out in the back of the room for sales. If you are at a place that doesn't allow sales of products in the lecture room after your speaking event, or there just isn't time, have a handout with your products that the attendees can fill out and meet you in the hallway to purchase what they want.

Having the ability to take credit cards on your smartphone or tablet will make this process easier. You can then either ship the items, email links, or if you have rented a booth at the event, have the customer meet you back at your booth to pick up their items.

Maintaining and Growing Customers Through Relationships

LISA   Your job as a business owner is to focus on the customer, both by bringing in new customers but also tending to existing customers and even more so, taking care of your loyal long-time customers. Here are some ways you can address each group of customers.

New Customers

LISA   Your newly acquired customer pool is your most active group. These customers have just discovered you and were convinced to purchase from you. They are more likely to purchase again than someone who just met you and didn't make a purchase.

You'll want to quickly take advantage of a new customer's attention by letting them know about the next level of products or services you have to offer. In Chapter 2 we discussed how it is important to focus on one thing as your main business, but that didn't mean to throw away the other ancillary things you may want to do in your spiritual business. Here is a good place to go back to those other things you offer and see what you can add to your spectrum of goods and services that can enhance your main business focus.

One of the add-on courses I teach is a basic crystal class, which I have found is very popular because people love crystals. This book is an outgrowth of a course I teach called "How To Start Your Spiritual Business." I began teaching that course because I had so many people ask me what I did to start my spiritual business both in-person and online, how I used the Internet for my business, and specific questions about getting a spiritual business up online.

If you are just starting out you may not have customers making requests for you to offer other things yet, but you can certainly draw on what you already know and what your other related interests are to create additional services or products.

Existing Customers

LISA You can reward your existing customers by giving them discounts and special deals to encourage them to come back and become repeat customers. They will be the ones you worked hard for and dedicate your services to. I try to reward my existing customers with early notifications of upcoming events. Since they are on my list I can let them know early and give them discounts to sign up and purchase before a certain date. The more you purchase with me the bigger the discounts I give in the future.

Loyal Long-time Customers

LISA You will have a few people who are your long-time customers who are very loyal to you and come to every event you hold, or have consistently bought all of your products for an extended period of time. I like to give these customers "freebies" and the biggest discounts to say, "Thank you, I very much appreciate your staying with me."

This type of reward is also a great way to get your loyal customers involved and seen by your newer customers, which shows your business is thriving! Having new prospective customers see that others are participating in your business, buying from you, and loving your work or products creates a wonderful purchasing motivator called Social Proof.

Social Proof

LISA Social proof refers to how a person's behavior is influenced by others, particularly a group of people who are deemed knowledgeable. Being knowledgeable may merely be an experience a person had, for example someone who has been to a particular store and recommends it to others. Social proof is also called social influence.

We see this in effect most often when purchasing an item online that has customer reviews. If there are a large number of positive customer reviews for a product, it is more likely to be seen as a good product to buy, or perhaps even perceived as a superior product with a high likelihood of customer satisfaction after purchase.

It is a very powerful psychological phenomenon that motivates people's behavior. Have you ever found yourself getting on a line that you didn't need to be on, but you just queued up because it was there? That's social proof or social influence. Everyone else is doing it so I can or should too. You can use social proof to encourage potential customers to purchase from you.

CINDY I see social influence all the time in my own business. When I am offering psychic readings at a psychic fair or holistic event, I like to pre-book my first few appointments. People see me busy right off the start and assume that because I am busier than those psychics who aren't with clients, that I must be better.

I often end up being booked well into the afternoon. The idea that "busy means better" is not necessarily true. I am good, but the psychics I usually work with are good, too. It is simply the perception, the *social influence*, which makes people think the busy psychics are better. What really makes a good psychic is what clients say afterward about his or her readings.

SPIRITUAL BUSINESS TIP #39

The best way to get testimonials is to ask for them.

LISA By getting customer referrals and asking for testimonials you are building social proof for your business. The best way to get testimonials is to ask for them. Sometimes you can get a great testimonial from a customer who tells you how much they love your work. When they do, ask them if you can use their kind words as a testimonial. I have never had anyone say no.

The easiest testimonials are written and many times they come from an email or letter someone writes you. Then it is easy for you to just copy what they wrote. You will need to get permission from them to use their words publicly and remember to ask if you can use their name.

Some people will not want their first and last name used but may only allow their first name and last initial. If you are prepared after a class or event you can get an audio or video testimonial from someone who attended. The best time to ask is when those who seem to really be enjoying your product or service are raving about it to you.

Video testimonials are more powerful than written ones, and ones that indicate the first and last name of the person stating the testimonial are more powerful than those without a name. One important note about testimonials that claim results, the Federal Trade Commission (FTC) has rules and guidelines on how testimonials can be presented, particularly when there are claims made about a product.

Also, never make up a testimonial. Since Cindy and I are not experts on FTC regulations, it is best to do some research on your own.

One of the easiest ways to get a good word shared about your business is on social media. The more engagement you have with your loyal customers on social media the better, since they may be more willing to say good things about your business.

CINDY   Like Lisa, I have never had clients tell me I could not use their kind words as a testimonial. If a client is especially happy with his or her reading, I say that the best compliment is a testimonial. I ask the client to email me one. Sometimes they do, sometimes they don't.

I have seen an option on some online appointment services where you can ask for a testimonial and I am looking into it. An email is automatically sent after the session with a request for feedback. Also if you use Square for your credit card service, they allow for feedback. I think that is a marvelous idea. Be ready for feedback of all sorts, though. It takes a thick skin, but you can learn a lot from any type of feedback. I also love the idea of a video testimonial — what a powerful marketing tool!

SYNERGIZE – ONLINE WITH THE INTERNET

SPIRITUAL BUSINESS TIP #40

Synergizing with your customers breaks down into two areas: staying in front of people and offering more things for people to buy.

LISA   Synergizing with your customers and potential customers on the Internet breaks down into two areas: offering more things for people to buy and staying in front of people.

Growing Your Business With Online Products and Services

LISA   Synergizing by using the Internet is easy to do because you don't have to leave your home to do it. Some businesses are easily able to provide services or products over the Internet. Other businesses still require that you meet your customer face-to-face.

Online, you can reach people frequently and on their time schedule, wherever they might be. These online products provide extra value to your customer that they may want to pay for.

For example, you may be an acupuncturist and an upsell product online you could offer could be an instruction booklet on what food supplements are good for certain common ailments people see acupuncturists for.

Here are some ways different spiritual businesses may be able to provide online products and services and take advantage of using the Internet. As an intuitive reader, coach, or counselor, for example, you may be able to do your consultations online with Skype, or through a video conference call on the web.

In any spiritual business, you might want to offer ways people can learn from you. People love to know more, and this can be done through webinars, telecasts, podcasts, and written material that can easily be provided as an added product online.

If you have a business where you do consultations you can offer add-on online services such as providing a written report, worksheets, "how-to lists," video instruction to follow up with your recommendations, or other supporting materials after the consultation. These items can be created as templates or as general materials that you commonly provide as part of your consultation.

Say you are a meditation facilitator; you may have recordings of your meditations that your customers can purchase as an online download. Even if you have a brick-and-mortar store you can set up an online store, have people order products over the Internet, and then simply ship them their goods.

CINDY Online upsells are easy to arrange, especially the lower tier or free upsells. You can put PDFs, support documents, videos and audio files on your website on a hidden page then send the client a link to the site or have them sign in to a members-only section of your site that requires a password.

Online Classes

LISA If your business centers on teaching or giving seminars and workshops, you can also do those online. I have created online courses for several years now, but only recently has the technology used to create online classes become so user friendly. The technology has advanced enough to be easier for customers to use and is secure enough to protect your material from being stolen.

Because of this, my latest online class was just as successful as my in-person class. The nice thing about offering an online class is that people who cannot afford the expense and time to travel can take my "How to Start Your Spiritual Business" and "Developing Your Intuition" courses anywhere, at any time. Online classes are normally done through what is known as a membership site where a student joins the site and becomes a member to take the online class.

The membership site is integrated with an online shopping cart, which can take payments online. The site handles all the security and login credentials to make sure that only those who have paid for the class have access to it.

CINDY I truly think online classes are the way our culture is moving for its educational needs. People are less afraid to give their credit card information online and more comfortable with the technology used for online classes. With websites and social media, prospective clients can come from anywhere on the globe. We have truly entered a global economy.

Online Stores

LISA You can easily now create an online store for these downloadable products. Many people are now publishing their own books and selling them online as an electronic document.

For example, you can compile interviews that you've done for your podcast and sell those as a package. Remember, all these products make great bonus incentives as well! You can give these as a bonus or part of a larger package to increase the value of what you are selling.

Webinars and Teleseminars/Teleconferences

LISA Meeting with your customers through virtual group gatherings can be done through what's known as a webinar where people can join a seminar over a web browser, hence the name "webinar."

Some webinars allow participants to also call in over the phone on a simultaneous conference call. Again people can join anytime and anywhere they wish, as long as they have access to the Internet or telephone. You can also do an Internet broadcast of a class that you are giving in person and therefore be able to include people who could not be there in person.

Remember, everything you do to get out there and serve your customer is a way to get in front of them, whether they are ready to purchase or not, or have purchased from you. As you create your products and services keep in mind the three types of customer tiers: new customers, existing customers, and long-time customers; and the three tiers of upsells: low, middle, and high.

Being in Front of People – Stay Connected With Technology

LISA Synergizing with people online to stay in front of them is now very easy with social media. Even though these activities may not be income producing such as selling a product or service it is a good form of advertising.

But more importantly, it is a way to continue to build your relationship with your customers, help build trust, and keep your business in the fore-front of their minds. Staying in front of people and keeping them engaged whether they are passive or actively engaging with you is very important.

Some people become frustrated with social media. They feel that no one is listening or paying attention because they don't have as much interaction as they would have expected. But just keep in mind that many people are passive and would prefer to just read rather than get involved. This is okay because it may take them a while to feel comfortable and speak up.

One way to get more interaction is to actually ask for it. Ask your readers to post or to reply. People do not want to be the first one to say something or to post, but if someone else starts, others will join in.

You can continue to connect with people through email, social media, forms of writing, video and audio that we've mentioned before in previous chapters to also synergize with your audience.

SPIRITUAL BUSINESS TIP #41

Make sure you write using a conversational tone. It is easier to read and people will feel more engaged with you.

SYNERGIZE – IN PERSON AND
THE TRADITIONAL WAY

LISA Some people prefer the in-person connection instead of being on-line. To synergize with these people you will have to find ways to make public appearances. Connecting in person is still very powerful, again, because we are social creatures. Also there is a segment of the population that does not have a computer for one reason or another.

There are also people who do not want to be on the computer or do not know how to use the technology. This group of people is best served in a non-technical way. The advantage of being in person is it can be a more powerful social interaction. The disadvantage of being in person is that you can only reach so many people at a time and it may require traveling and renting space. The more people you want to reach, the more you have to travel and that can be expensive.

If your business is conducted in person then connecting that way is probably the best way for you to stay in front of your customers. Your business will most likely be local, and you'll want to meet as many people as you can locally.

Lectures, Speaking, and Giving Talks

LISA   Being face-to-face with people is a great way to synergize with them. You can do this by speaking, giving a lecture or a workshop. Now for some people public speaking is difficult because they are afraid of speaking in front of a group.

As mentioned earlier, if you are nervous speaking in public, you can join a Toastmasters group or maybe ask some friends to let you practice in front of them. If you're not afraid of speaking in front of people then giving a talk is a great way to stay in front of your customer. As we spoke about earlier it is also a great way to attract customers.

You can give talks or lectures at expos, healing fairs and other people's group events. Many times companies are looking for outside speakers to add value to their internal corporate events. When you are first starting out doing talks you will probably have to pay a fee to speak at an event.

If you become very good at speaking, and probably after a lot of experience, you may be paid to do your talk. Of course the best way to generate a crowd is to talk for free.

Lectures or talks are sometimes done with event holders where you split the price of the tickets that people pay to come listen. Other times you may be asked to speak but not be paid for it even though the audience has paid to attend. What you gain from public speaking, from the event holder, is exposure to a new audience that may become your new customers.

Classes and Workshops

LISA   Whether or not giving classes and workshops is a main part of your business, giving a class or workshop can be really good for synergizing with your customer. Anytime that you are educating your customer on topics that are relevant to your business you're engaging them to learn more about how your business can help them.

What makes a class or workshop different from a lecture is that the class or workshop is more interactive. You might have exercises or handouts or even samples to give out during the class.

If you normally teach or give seminars as the main part of your business, you can also give mini-classes or mini-workshops, which might be more affordable on an ongoing basis.

Classes that meet once a week, or perhaps for a shorter period like a series of classes for a six-week period provide similar opportunities to synergize and also can be an additional product offering.

CINDY There are few better ways to create *synergy* with your clients than offering them free or low-cost information in the form of a class or workshop. My free monthly lecture series, "Metaphysics Interactive," was not only my way to give back to my community, it was a way to show my expertise and be in front of my clientele once a month. My students felt they were getting valuable information free, and in return, I received their loyalty.

Special Group Gatherings

LISA Another way to provide "extras" to your customers in order to keep them synergizing with you is to offer special group gatherings. You can create special events like retreats, a field trip, or even a social gathering. These all provide a way for clients or customers to stay in touch with you, be engaged with the things you're offering, and build your relationship.

You can hold a retreat at a spiritual center or a small hotel and give your customers a deep immersion experience. This provides another offering for your customers and gives them a more in-depth way to get to know you, and spend time with you in your work.

I have led a retreat called "Sedona's Sacred Places" in which I take a group to all the famous metaphysical sacred sites that Sedona, Arizona, is known for. Leading a retreat takes a lot of work, but it is a great way to get to know your customers and for them to get to know you, plus you have a great reason to get together and synergize.

Meetup.com is a very popular online site where people can sign up for meetings that you hold. These meetings tend to be for free and the website is meant to provide a place where like-minded people can get together and share their interests. I used Meetup.com for my Intuition Development Circle meetings, which were free at the time. The members of my group numbered over 150.

Another type of event you can hold to synergize with your customers is a field trip. For example I have taken groups of people on a field trip to the Saint Padre Pio shrine and to see St. Patrick's Cathedral which are both in New York City. It's a fun way to get your customers involved in a shared interest.

Snail Mailings

SPIRITUAL BUSINESS TIP #42

You want the money spent on snail mail to pay off. Keep your mailing short, with easy to read fonts and plenty of white space.

LISA   If email is not an option for your less technical clients, or you're not ready for mass emails, you can still use snail mail effectively. Cindy has much more experience with this and offers some great advice.

CINDY   Although there is a need to keep a good database, I do find snail mailings are well received and people actually read them. With snail mail, or USPS mail, you print up a document, stick it in an envelope, put a stamp on it, and mail it to your clients. As mentioned, email has its place and so does snail mail.

I am finding that as my business grows and my clientele becomes savvier, in a few years snail mail may very well become obsolete. Until then, you want the money you spend on snail mail to pay off. Often it is a temptation to overload the envelope, but it's important not to fall prey to this temptation.

Keep your documents short, with easy-to-read fonts and plenty of white space. I find a short cover letter or flyer along with a professionally made brochure works best. People tend to hold on to a professional brochure rather than a letter on a plain-white sheet of paper.

Building Your Snail Mail List

CINDY   I like to get both the client's street address and the email. My clients often change emails or write illegibly, so you can always send a note to the mailbox address if the email bounces. You don't want to take someone's home address without his or her knowledge. No one likes junk mail in the mailbox or the inbox. Once you get the addresses, you will need a good customer database.

For mailings, you need a customer database system that will generate labels and be easy to update. Using out-of-date addresses is like throwing money down the drain. I am always looking at an easier way to track my customers and keep my customer database up to date. Using contests, database forms, and sign-in sheets are the best way to get addresses.

Snail mailings are not a monthly thing. You should do one often enough to keep your addresses up to date, but two to four times a year is plenty.

You may even choose to mail out only once a year. When I am teaching a lot of classes locally, I might do a snail mailing twice a year to announce my teaching schedule for the spring and fall. My local target audience is smaller so snail mail is not cost-prohibitive. Also, a number of my students either do not use email, or if they do, sheepishly admit they don't check them often.

You'll need to figure out how much you would need to make to pay for the mailing. For example, let's say I am sending out a mailing for my spring classes and workshops. I have 100 people on my list, and using 2015 rates, stamps are 49 cents. Let's say I do a nice B&W brochure that I print at my local UPS store.

When you have an account you can get a good rate, so let's say 100 double-sided brochures cost me $8. I want to add a discount coupon for my psychic services, $2 to print those, and a cover letter with helpful hints for energetic spring cleaning. Good paper may run me about $10 and I print these on my home computer for a total cost of $14. Envelopes cost about $2; I buy mine at Staples or at a warehouse store. I use the free return address labels I get with donation solicitations.

Total cost of this mailing is about $72. If my classes are $25 per student, I need three students, or maybe just one reading from the discount card I included to pay for the mailing. Though I might not get three students from the mailing, each of my 100 local students has been reminded I am teaching spiritual classes, helping them perceive me as an expert on spiritual development, and as a psychic. They also get a discount coupon to entice them to use my services instead of someone else's!

It may be tempting to use bulk mail to save money, but unless you have a huge mailing it is time-consuming. It will cost more to get back bad addresses and forwarded addresses, if you get them back at all. Also, bulk mail gives your mailing a junk-mail appearance. You are much more likely to have your mail opened if it bears a first-class stamp, so splurge for the stamps and tell your clients that they are "first class" to you!

Blessing Your Mailing

CINDY   If you are going to spend all that time and money, what are a few extra minutes to bless your stack of envelopes or postcards before you send them? Mail them off with the best energy and intentions possible. When I am attaching labels, I actually say the person's name to myself while offering a blessing. I just say "Blessings, Sarah," or whatever the person's name is.

When I am all done, I then take a few moments and send some healing energy while I say the following blessing: "Please bless all who come in contact with this letter. Let them feel the positive and loving intention in which this mailing is sent."

LISA You can also bless your emails before you hit "Send." Energy works with everything, and follows your intent.

JOINT VENTURES – GROW YOUR BUSINESS TEN-FOLD THROUGH SHARING

LISA If you are a small business and solo entrepreneur, the best way to grow your business is to partner with other businesses. This may seem like selling out to the competition, but you are not. In the spiritual business world, working together should be natural, as we are all One, and in the spirit of that philosophy and practice, partnering should be easy. This kind of partnership is called a *joint venture*. By working together, you both benefit. It is a win-win situation.

What we can do as one business can be multiplied by doubling our resources and efforts for one another. By sharing your market reach and your resources, both of your businesses can reach more customers. Pursuing a joint venture is actually how many businesses have become successful.

Who to Share With?

> **SPIRITUAL BUSINESS TIP #43**
>
> Your best joint venture partners to share with are going to be those who either complement your business or who you consider to be your competitors.

LISA Your best joint venture partners to share with are going to be those who either complement your business or who you consider to be your competitors. Generally, you both are looking for the same types of customers, may already have a set of customers and if you promote each other's businesses, you've just doubled your potential customer base.

Say you are a chiropractor, you may partner with a massage therapist. Perhaps you are an acupuncturist, you may partner with an herbalist. If you are an intuitive reader, you may partner with an energy healer.

If you both realize the power of partnering and sharing your resources there should never be competition. The power truly is in the partnership!

How to Share
Shared Mailings and Advertising

CINDY   Other spiritual businesses are not your competition; they are your allies. Especially if you have spent time nurturing your relationships, you can work with different practitioners to market, educate, and service those in your community.

For example, I have often shared marketing with other teachers in my area who teach spiritual development. When I was teaching more, I used to put out a mailing with a fellow teacher. We were able to reach double the potential students than if we were marketing separately. That same friend now has her own spiritual center and I am teaching a class in her center as well as teaching a class across town. She has referred her students and clients to both of my classes.

You will find that shared mailings and advertising are both financially rewarding and the best way to reach the largest group of interested people. You will also find the resulting goodwill is a far-reaching benefit.

SPIRITUAL BUSINESS TIP #44

To grow your business astronomically, partner with other people in your same line of business.

Sharing the Work

LISA   There are many ways that you can work with your joint venture partners by sharing the work that you both do. You can share events, classes, or webinars where you both can be presenters, or perhaps you can split the work based on what each of you is best at.

Maybe one of you is better at presenting and the other is better at organizing. One of you can be the presenter and the other can do all the paperwork and management of getting the event together. In fact it might be easier for you to start out with a partner in doing an event or class.

You can also share webinars or teleseminars online, which may be even easier since you don't have to rent a space or leave your home. You can even try partnering with someone to write a book, just as Cindy and I did on this book.

CINDY   Everyone has his or her own strengths. My frequent joint venture partner, Virginia, jokes that my control issues work well for her. She and I brainstorm ideas together and then I do all the rest. It works well for both of us.

Shared Contests

CINDY Shared contests create a bigger buzz than one you might do on your own. The more prizes in a contest, the more appealing it is; the more contestants, the more significant the impact. Ask a few practitioners to offer prizes and promotion for your joint venture contest and all involved will share the contacts and goodwill gained.

My husband and I are part of the Upstate New York IANDS group that has bi-monthly meetings. We used to offer just one book in a raffle. Then one of our board members started donating two framed photographs with channeled sayings. So now we have three things in the raffle and as a result get a lot more people to buy tickets! When doing a shared contest, the benefits increase exponentially.

When starting out, teaching with a more experienced person is an outstanding way to increase your knowledge, talent, and client base. You can also offer shared events where you and another, or group of others, offer your services.

For example, I do a holiday open houses at two different local New Age centers. It works for all of us as we cross promote through each other's email lists and by social networking. Also, it builds fellowship and camaraderie. Many of my referrals come from people I have worked alongside with in the spiritual community. Working together with your colleagues turns competition into opportunities!

LISA Cindy is right on about sharing your events and collaborating with colleagues. There is power and reach in joining forces with others that you may have thought were your competitors. They can be your allies and, in fact, when creating that team work you both win and can generate much more income for each other than if you were alone.

CINDY Using Lisa's "Attract, Resonate, and Synergize" should have your business booming in no time. Yet we cannot understate the importance of professional promotional material. To help you create the most compelling promotion you can, Lisa and I next offer you our secrets for great promotional copywriting and design.

CHAPTER EIGHT

Creating Enticing Promotional Material

· · · · · · · · · · · · · · · ·

SPIRITUAL BUSINESS TIP #45

Promotional materials need to follow one basic rule. Professional, Professional, Professional!

LISA Promoting your business is one of the most important things you must do to grow and sustain your business. This is pretty much what we've been talking about the last three chapters. If I haven't convinced you yet, I will say it again: without marketing, your business will not survive.

Most of us would like to have a product that sells itself but realistically there are no products that sell themselves. Since you need to market then you'll want to create the most compelling promotional material you can make. Great promotional material has two components; one is how it looks and, more importantly, what it says in the text.

Humans are visual creatures; therefore the visual appeal of your graphics is key in attracting initial attention. The words used to describe and convey your message will tap into the second important piece, which is human emotion. How you write your marketing material will determine how long you hold someone's attention and eventually get people to purchase.

CINDY Promotional materials for a spiritual business need to follow a basic rule: Professional, Professional, Professional! Your most essential promotional asset is your website. Many different options are available for building your website; you can use a traditional website or even a blog as long as you keep it professional-looking and easy to navigate.

Next in importance will be your "hard copy" marketing materials, such as brochures, flyers, postcards, and business cards. Thanks to online printing services, these marketing materials can be made up easily and at low cost. There is no reason to skimp on any of your promotional material.

CAPTURING ATTENTION AND KEEPING IT

LISA What if I told you that the very first time I ever gave a talk for the public there was standing room only? Would you like to hear how intuition saved my life after I developed my intuition from scratch? Do you want to know how I got strangers to spend thousands of dollars to take my course by just seeing one of my online videos? Wouldn't you want to hear more?

All of the answers to these questions are true and each has a story behind them. Compelling promotional material and marketing begins with presenting something that someone wants and then telling a story that leads someone to want to pursue, through your business, getting that something.

It is also about how you tell the story. Suppose I then told you that the talk I gave packed the room with only 5 words? Now I really have your attention. Why? Because, I assume that you're reading this book because you want to improve your business. That you want to be able to attract more people to your business and get them to spend money with you. My stories peaked your curiosity so you want to hear more.

Your wants and my offer to show you how you can get what you want is capturing your attention and compelling you to want to hear more. Addressing someone's wants attracts attention by connecting to his or her emotion of desire. Curiosity is naturally captivating.

Copywriting That's Worth 1,000 Words

LISA When you are writing promotional material, you are now in the realm of "copywriting speak." Copywriting is defined as the text written for advertising or publicity.

Copywriting is a style of writing that is short on words but catches someone's attention and holds it while motivating him or her to take action. That action can be to do something to find out more, it can be clicking on a button to buy a service or product, it might be picking up the phone to call a business, or it may just be signing up to be on an email list so they can receive more information in the future.

Even though copywriting looks like it is short and easy it can take a lot of time to write. What can help you write your copy is to truly understand the desires of your target market. This requires that you get into their "heads," so to speak. It may not be too difficult for you to do because you might have been in their position at one time.

Good copywriting takes practice to write. The shorter your copy the longer it will take for you to write it. So don't get discouraged if your copy does not sound great at first. You may want to pick up a book on copywriting just to educate yourself on how it's done. Remember that copywriting also includes titles. These may be titles of your class or workshop, of the talk you are giving, or of an article you are writing.

You should be thinking about writing titles, descriptions, advertisements and any promotional material as a form of copywriting.

Good copywriting attracts attention and draws your audience in. The first step is to understand your audience and who is your target market. When you know your audience well you know how to write for them. The important thing is to know what they want and how you can help them get it. Generally you'll want to write in a way that people can easily understand you, which is going to be less formal and more colloquial.

It is important to get away from the corporate speak because people generally do not listen carefully to something they cannot personally relate to or cannot understand easily. You would like to make people feel that they are in a conversation with you in a way that makes sense. Here's an example of what is too impersonal:

"Our business model implements a systematic approach to help businesses organize and optimize their processes to improve efficiency in their results, increase dependable income streams and maximize revenue flow."

I'm not even sure I know what that means. Now, here is my copy that is more conversational, and easier to understand:

"Does your spiritual business offer lots of things to buy but no one seems to be purchasing? Hi I'm Lisa K., and I can show you three easy steps that will help you pick the best product to offer that gets more people to buy, and buy from you and only you, more often."

I would gather that the second copy is easier for you to follow and may be a bit more compelling than the first.

Copywriting is a large subject, so we'll just touch on it here and give you highlights. The best thing is to read a book on copywriting so you can improve your skill in making your writing persuasive. The key take-away here for copywriting is to know your potential customers and what they commonly want and then provide them a solution for getting what they want.

Here's an example. I'm sure you're wondering how I was able to pack a room to standing room only. I packed the room with only five words... and they were the words for the title of my talk.

My business is teaching people how to develop their intuition. I know that my potential customers want a stronger intuition than they have control over, and that the most common question they ask is: "How do I know it's my intuition and not me making it up?" The talk that packed the room was called, "10 Key Secrets to Intuition."

The title addresses the seemingly elusive understanding of what intuition is, that it's almost secretive, and this talk will reveal the secrets to understanding it. The word "Key" indicates that these secrets are important to know. My potential customers also want to know these secrets to intuition, because intuition is a mystery to them. I always use the word *intuition* instead of psychic abilities because most people believe they can be intuitive but not necessarily psychic.

How did I know all this? I surveyed my potential customers and my existing customers. I always ask, "What is your biggest issue regarding your intuition?" I also ask, "How many of you think you are intuitive?" and then, "How many of you believe you are or could be psychic?"

Through the answers to these questions, I discovered what my customers want and desire. My talk title, and then my description, targets this desire and provides a way for them to get what they want. By the way, the video of this talk is also what motivated people to spend thousands of dollars to take my in-person course, even though they hadn't met me.

In the video I tell the story of how intuition saved my life. If you'd like to see the video, go to YouTube and search for *"10 Key Secrets to Intuition Lisa K."*

Graphic Arts Is Looking Good and First Impressions

LISA I'm not an artist, and I don't consider myself particularly good at visual arts, but I recognize the importance of good graphics in promotional material. That being said, I really enjoy using graphics and pictures in my newsletters, which I pick myself. It gives me a great opportunity to exercise my right brain, where both our visual creativity and intuition comes from. The graphics you use in your promotional material gives a first impression that can either attract or repel. Most of us are attracted to visual things first.

Pictures and graphics also convey a feeling and emotion that is received instantly. When picking graphics, it is important to pay attention to how the graphic makes you feel. Again, it is a great way to practice using your intuition as well. Which picture is attractive to you? Is it giving you the impression that you would like to convey? Is there an unsaid message in the picture that you want to express in your marketing material?

The first impression will usually come from the graphics you use. If the impression is bad or poor, people will think badly or poorly of your material. Say your business is about promoting relaxation, stress reduction and calmness. In this case you may not want to use a graphic that has an angry, chaotic or loud feel to it.

Choose graphics that are inviting and not cluttered. Pick colors that are attractive. Of course, not everyone will feel exactly the same about the same picture or photograph, but there are commonalities in the impression one will give the onlooker.

There are many free resources for graphics and images online that you can use even for commercial purposes. There are many places where you can purchase a license to use stock images for promotional material.

You must make sure you have permission to use an image that you did not create. To use someone else's photo, picture, graphic, image or drawing without their permission violates copyright law. These laws may differ for every country or even state. Some companies who own images will go after you legally for using their images without permission. A list of resources for images you can license for a fee or free is in Resources.

Copyright law also covers images used in social media, so make sure you have permission to use an image if it is not one you have created yourself. Be careful of taking photographs of artwork, brands or people's faces and then using them since you may be violating copyright or privacy laws.

The best thing to do is to use a stock photo supplier that can provide you with a license to use the image, either for a fee or in some cases for free with an attribution to the creator and/or supplier. If you purchase an image from a supplier your rights are usually not transferable. That means you cannot give those images to others to use on their marketing material.

Images and graphics can be strong attractors to your promotional material, so choosing the right ones is essential. Make sure the images are conveying the impression, feeling and emotion you want to convey. Take your time in choosing the right image. You can also ask others for their feedback on the images you choose if you feel you aren't sure how others will react to it.

Riveting Storytelling

LISA People love stories and you may not think you are a good story-teller, but truly we all have some ability to tell a story. We're often telling stories when we get together with our friends and gossip. We are telling a story when we are describing what happened to us the other day.

Humans are psychologically geared to tell stories, listen to stories, and love them. Stories are entertaining, engaging, illustrative and memorable.

When I teach a two full-day class that is full of information, the things that people remember the most are the stories I tell. For this reason I tell lots of stories. People also want to hear stories about other people, particularly a story about the storyteller.

When you first meet someone you want to know about who he or she is, where the person is from and how he or she got here. *You would like to hear their story.* When someone starts to tell a story, people automatically become quiet and listen. You can use stories in your copywriting or marketing material to hold on to your audience's attention and keep them listening.

I often tell a story about how my intuition saved my life. It's a true story, and by the way, you should always tell true stories. It was a scary event that had a good ending, so the story evokes emotion. What is compelling about this is not just that it is my story, but it demonstrates how I was able to develop my intuition from scratch where I developed control over it to use it when I needed to.

I knew it was my intuition giving me information that I listened to and acted on, to save my life. This addresses a "customer want," which is wanting to know how to tell their intuition is giving them a message and it was not their minds making it up.

I demonstrate, through my story, that I was able to start at a point where they are now, and that is developing my intuition from scratch. Even further, I was able to develop my intuition to such a high degree that I used it in a time of crisis to avert disaster.

The story helps people see that they can be like me and it's possible to get what they want, which is use their intuition on what they want, when they want.

Here then is my story about how my intuition saved my life:

I've learned how to develop my intuition from scratch. In the beginning, using my intuition was terrible, I didn't know how to hear it or connect with it, nor even know when it was happening inside me. Through studying, learning and practicing I developed my intuition until one day my intuition saved my life.

One night I woke up shaking uncontrollably. I couldn't even hold a glass of water in my hand and I knew something was very wrong. My husband called the ambulance and they took me to the hospital. The emergency room doctors did a routine blood test and found I had bacteria in my blood, but they told me, "You're not shaking anymore, go home see your doctor in the morning."

I went to my doctor the next morning and he did what doctors normally do; he gave me antibiotic pills. I took the medication but it didn't help. Every day I would have bouts of my heart racing and shortness of breath even though I was lying down in bed. I couldn't understand why this was happening and it definitely didn't feel right.

It happened again, only this time it was so bad I thought I was going to pass out and my hands turned white. I went to the emergency room again. This time I told the doctor, "It's getting worse, I'm short of breath and my heart is pounding, my hands turned white, what is that?" The doctor replied, "Oh, you were hyperventilating, that was fear." I told him, "I really don't think so. I think this is something more than that." But the doctor persisted and said, "No, just go home, continue to take your medicine and you'll be fine."

So at this point my intuition is telling me that this is not right and something is very wrong. I turned within and the intuitive messages that I received were that I really need to find an infectious disease specialist and then I will be okay.

This was over the weekend and you can't find a doctor over the weekend. I didn't know what to do. The bouts were continuing to get worse. I was then guided by my intuition to read a particular book on how to find the best pediatrician amongst many books on my bookshelf. I didn't know why at the time, but I started to read it. As I read the book, of course the word pediatrician kept coming up over and over again. I thought, "Wait a minute, my pediatrician is my friend and he's my neighbor. Maybe he knows of someone who could help me."

As I go to pick up the phone and just before I dial, in my head my intuition pops this message, "He's away on vacation but he'll be back later so leave a detailed message." I dial the phone and when he didn't pick up, I left a detailed message. Later that afternoon he called me back and said, "I was away on vacation, I just came home and got your message. I know exactly what you need to do, you need to see an infectious disease specialist and I know one who will see you right away. I am going to email him now and he will see you."

The next day I called this doctor and he saw me immediately. He took more blood tests and when the results came back, he said, "Yes, we have more information, not only do you have bacteria in your blood but you also have a heart infection." He then put me in the hospital.

Long story short, fortunately I received six weeks of the proper treatment and he cured me. I realized, had I not gotten the intuitive messages to get help right away and to not listen to those other doctors that were saying "You're okay just go home," I don't know whether I'd be here today.

Having a blood infection is very serious and can be fatal. A heart infection, or endocarditis, is also very bad. The doctors and I were relieved that I didn't have any heart damage from it.

I thank my intuition for saving my life. This is the main reason I teach others to develop their intuition, because it can help them in big and important ways in their life, as mine has for me.

What is your story? Do you have a story that is related to your business? It does not have to be a story about an event in your life. It can be a story about your helping someone get what he or she wanted through your work. The stories can be from testimonials or results your customers had from using your product or service.

Use your stories in your copywriting or marketing material to hold your audience's attention and keep them listening.

ENTICING PROMOTIONAL MATERIALS
Your Business Website

SPIRITUAL BUSINESS TIP #46

Your most essential promotional asset is your website.

LISA One of the most efficient ways to present yourself to the public is through your website. It is a promotional piece that works for you, often for free or little cost, 24 hours a day seven days a week, all the time, at any time!

You can put up as much information about yourself, your business and products as you wish. As Cindy will explain later, it is important that you don't crowd your home page with volumes of information, you can have other pages on your website to elaborate and organize your business services and descriptions.

Your most compelling copywriting that describes both your business and yourself should be on the home page of your website. Remember to think about what your customer wants and desires to accomplish or get in life. Then describe how your business can provide that. Because your home page is the first thing people will look at, and will be your biggest promoter, it is important that you focus your efforts on creating a page that is pleasing to look at, ie., you should be proud to display it.

Include a concise and persuasive paragraph that will make people want to read more. This short paragraph or paragraphs should contain your "elevator" pitch, which is short enough to explain who you are and what you do. This should entice people to want to read more and click on your services or product descriptions.

Websites are powerful marketing tools because you can be descriptive both through words and images. Images are what attracts most people's attention, so having a good banner or featured image at the top of each of your website pages is important. It pulls together all of your web pages.

My website banner contains my branding, which is my business name "Lisa K." and my logo. My banner was created by a professional graphic artist and I use the banner on both my main website and my membership site where my students participate in my online classes. This helps "sew" together my sites so they have the same theme. When people see my banner or logo, they know it's connected to my business.

Your website may have just your business name or your photograph to identify your business. If you have a brick-and-mortar location, you may have a photograph of your business storefront so you can be easily located. If you are a one-person business, don't be afraid to put up a photograph of yourself. Even if you are just offering your services, customers want to know who they are buying their services from.

I am actually a shy person when it comes to putting my face up publically, but I realized that it is important for people to be able to see me. They will see you eventually if you buy from you. As we mentioned before, you can get a professional set of headshots that will be more flattering than having a friend take your photograph. So promote your business by promoting you!

The next most important page on your site after your home page is your "About" page. An About page is where you describe your business and yourself. If you have a brick-and-mortar business like a store or practice with several practitioners, you will want to describe your business as a whole, and may want to include a short description of the owner.

If your business is just you providing services, then you'll want your About page to be about you. Remember, this page is also promoting you, so writing good copy is important.

Don't forget, contact information is important because you want potential customers to easily find you once you've gotten their interest. Remember to include, how to find you and where. I have a contact form that reaches me instantly if you fill it out and a way you can call me. If you do have a customer contact you, respond right away, otherwise they may think your business is not active.

SPIRITUAL BUSINESS TIP #47

Most people will not wait for a slow webpage to load.

CINDY Lisa and I have shared a lot of information about websites throughout this book, but still I will add a few points on tech matters. It is important for the website to be easy to read on old or new computers and good and bad Internet connections.

As I am writing this, I am in the Dominican Republic with lousy Internet service. Some website pages just don't want to open. Believe it or not, I still know people who use dial-up. Yes, in 2015! If you load each page on your website with too many graphics, some people will give up on your page as it takes too long to load. Most people with high-speed Internet are willing to wait about 5 seconds for a page to load, people on slow connections may wait 20 seconds.

As you develop your website, there are often ways, either within the website building software or with online programs such as Speedtest.net, to test your page at different Internet speeds and on different browsers. So choose low-resolution pictures that load quickly, easy-to-read fonts, simple navigation, and provide plenty of "white space."

Avoid one long page, unless you use what are called "anchors" to take the client from the top of the page to a lower section. A long or crowded page is not only difficult to navigate — it is not going to look professional and will take longer to load. Take the time to look at websites of practitioners you respect. They don't have to be from the same occupation. Soon you'll see what works and what doesn't.

Make sure to have your contact information on every page, as your clients may not look too hard for your phone number or email. You might want to think of the website as an expanded press kit, but here you can expand on each section with details. We will discuss how to create a press kit later in this chapter. Don't forget to put your digital press kit on your website, too!

Lead Pages and Autoresponders in Email Marketing

LISA The way to get people to give you their email address so you can promote your business to them is through what is known as a "lead page" and an autoresponder.

A lead page is a simple website page that has a form on it to capture a visitor's information on that form and has no other information on that page other than to urge people to fill out the form. For example, I have a lead page that only asks for an email address and says simply, "Sign up to be the first to know when Developing Your Intuition Online opens to the public! Develop Your Intuition so you can make it happen when you want, on what you want and get detailed information."

Then there is a box to put in only an email address and click a button that says, "Get on the list!" It's short, simple and those people who are interested sign up. Because I'm not asking for too much information, there is less resistance by visitors to give their email address. The great thing about a simple lead page like this is that it creates a list that is "self selected."

I know the people who signed up for this list are mainly interested in my course. I can then make sure that they are the ones that I push all information regarding my course to, since they asked for it.

An autoresponder is an email that is automatically sent out to the person who signed up for a list to say thank you, to give follow-up information or to provide the promised "gift" for signing up. Email marketing services will have an autoresponder feature build into their systems that you can turn on and use.

The autoresponder can be triggered in a variety of ways. The most common autoresponder is to be triggered when someone signs up on a list. Other complex ways you can use an autoresponder is having it triggered when someone clicks on a link on your website, purchases a product from you or perhaps send out a happy birthday message on a customer's birthday.

These autoresponders can be a very powerful way to keep connected with your customer without your having to lift a finger. That being said, I would not use just autoresponders to email customers, but have a mix of autoresponders and emails sent out as I create them. The most common autoresponder is used to send out a promised "gift" for signing up.

On my website, if you sign up for my list you will get a free eBook on developing your intuition which has 16 intuition exercises you can do by yourself.

Brochures

SPIRITUAL BUSINESS TIP #48

People read headings; they rarely read the paragraph below it.

CINDY Brochures are meant to give detailed information, yet common mistakes I see are too many words and not enough white space, crazy fonts and colors, or using too many fonts and colors. Here are some hints for creating a good brochure:

- Avoid clip art and crazy colors. Stars and moons may have been your favorite as a child, but you may find them looking childish as a brochure background.
- Remember: white space. Most people don't like to read a lot, so if there are too many words and no space between them, they won't bother.
- Look at other people's brochures for ideas. Don't copy, it's rude and dishonest, but you can get some good ideas for what works and what does not work.
- Once you have created your brochure, print it out and have someone look at it who will be honest with you.

The headings for each paragraph should be easy to understand yet interesting. "Services" may describe what you are offering but it is kind of bland as a heading. Try something creative and descriptive, but not cliché. People read headings; they rarely read the paragraph below until after they have decided the information is worth a second look.

Use the information you created in the second chapter about what is different about your service, the benefits, and how your service transforms. Here is where your earlier effort pays off! You already have short paragraphs, or better yet, bullet points about what you do, how you are unique, the benefits of your work, etc. If you are skimming this page, you probably stopped to read the bullet points above.

Avoid using more than two different type fonts. Also, if your brochure's font size is too big it will look childish, and fonts that are too small are hard to read and just plain inconsiderate! In a brochure, depending on the font chosen, 11-or 12-point is good for paragraphs and 12-or 14-point for headings. You might choose a bigger font on the cover to attract attention.

Avoid lots of colors in your fonts. Limit colors to 2 or 3 if you are doing a color brochure. There is nothing wrong with a black and white brochure, but you might want to print it on heavier stock, or better, colored stock. You can buy pre-printed brochure paper online that is ready for your printer. You can print in black to save money while still having a colorful brochure. I like to use Paperdirect.com, but search online for other alternatives.

Finally, make a few test copies after you design your brochure. I guarantee you will want to make changes. I recommend finding a nice brochure paper, sold online, or use a color paper and print them either at home or at a local place that does copies. It may cost you more for the first 25, but it costs more in the long run to print 500 and then decide you want to make changes.

Flyers

CINDY Flyers are for promoting a special event, new product, or new service. Color flyers are great, that is, if you can actually read the flyer. Yes, that dark sunset background is stunning, but with dark-color ink, no one can read what the flyer says! Use a font that people can read and, as with brochures, make sure the flyer is visually appealing with lots of white space, bullets to show benefits of your service, and include your contact information.

It still amazes me when I get a flyer and can't easily find the contact information or can't read the pretty but unintelligible fancy font. With flyers, don't try to put in every detail. I provide an email, phone number, and website for more information, whereas Lisa usually simply puts the website and sometimes a phone number.

A good flyer uses tantalizer bullets to get readers' attention, giving them enough information so they know the what, where, when, and how much, as well as how to contact you for more information. Most people prefer going to a website for more information rather than calling, but include both the website and phone number.

A flyer is a perfect example of why you want an easy-to-remember website name. People don't always take the flyer with them and will have to remember your contact information. The longer or more difficult the name, the more likely they won't get to your site and you won't get their business.

Postcards

CINDY Online printers are always offering deals on postcards. I like postcards for mailing, but I print my own postcards at a local UPS store on yellow cardstock, four to a page, and cut them with a paper cutter.

It's cheaper than buying online as I can print only the number I need. Many people are turning to double sided, over-sized display postcards printed on heavy stock that is not meant for mailing. I don't find they work well at events like psychic fairs and wellness events.

Some swear by postcards, and I like them for an upcoming event or to promote a new service. But I have found that prospective clients often want more details than a postcard can provide. Each type of marketing material has its use, and through trial and error you'll find what works best for your clientele.

Postcards follow the same rules as brochures and flyers as far as white space, colors, and fonts go, but large graphics work well here. I like to use over-sized display postcards if I am not mailing them because I can make the front look snazzy and glossy, while putting the real information on the back in simple black and white print.

Mailing postcards work well as reminders, but you can't put much information on them. I use them when I want to let my clients know I am going to be at a psychic fair or holistic event and I include an incentive discount. Postcard stamps cost less than mailing an envelope and you can almost guarantee recipients will at least look at it to see what it is. In contrast, you have to hope your client will open an envelope or email.

LISA My printed promotional material is usually limited to postcards or rack cards. I like these marketing materials because they are bigger than a business card, can be very attractive, and have enough space for more information. Since they are made with thicker material than just regular paper, they hold up to people taking them and looking at them with one hand, then shoving into a purse, bag or pocket.

Also, when someone passes by you can easily hand them a card if they seem interested in finding out more about you or a product. Rack Cards are like postcards but are half the size of a piece of an 8.5 x 11-inch letter-sized piece of paper lengthwise, but they are made with card stock. Both postcards and rack cards are the perfect size to place in a plastic rack holder that you can buy at an office supply store.

If you go to a public event, fair or expo, bring your promotional materials and a holder or stand to place them in. When I give a talk, or do an event, I can display the cards in special holders for people to pick up. I've discovered that when I do an event such as an expo or fair there are often tables where you can place your promotional material. Since for these events I do not always have my own table, this is a way to promote my business beyond my talk.

These tables might have other people's flyers and cards there as well and you would like yours to stand out. Many attendees pick these materials up because it's almost as if it's a freebie that they would like to collect. Most vendors just have their cards, brochures and flyers laid out flat, but if you have a plastic holder that stands up for your material, it is easier for attendees to see and pick up so yours will stand out among the others.

I will also print out a "mini-poster" that is 8.5 x 11 inches on plain paper and put it in a plastic stand to place on a table. This mini-poster can be printed portrait or landscape orientation.

CINDY I have just started using rack cards and am very excited about them because of their shape and height. Regular postcards are short and wide; they don't stand out even if you purchase a stand for them. Rack cards fit perfectly in a traditional brochure holder and will stand out more than the flyers and cards lying on a table.

The brochure holder often gets "removed" if it becomes empty so I tape my business card on the front to deter people from using it for their material. They aren't expensive; so don't avoid using one just because it might not be there when you get back. It is worth the investment.

LISA Having images on your postcards is always attractive. If a card only has text on it the card will not be as enticing. Always make sure to put your name, contact information and website on the card because people may not remember where they got the card from.

The copywriting that you put on your card should be short and compelling. The layout on your card should not be crowded. I like to use online printing services because they are relatively inexpensive compared to a brick-and-mortar print shop. Also, it is very convenient because they'll often have templates to get you started.

The templates look very professional and often already have selected images that you can use. Another nice thing about using online print services is that you do not have to order thousands of pieces. What you can do is start with a smaller amount, for example 25 to 50 and see how well they attract attention.

If you are just starting out, your business description may change as you hone your copywriting skills, so you do not want to have a large amount of printed material you would have to throw out later if the description no longer applies. Another great thing about online printing services is they are very professional and the products that they provide are top quality, giving a very professional look. You can also print in color on one side or both and they offer a variety of card stock you can use such as matte finish or glossy.

From my experience I have found that these cards do work. I've had a few people who came to me later for a reading or other service say they couldn't attend my lecture but took my postcard to follow up with me. One great thing about any printed material you create is, in their own way, they keep you in front of a person. Have you ever gotten someone's card or brochure and left it on your desk, then kept seeing it there day after day?

Promoting yourself and marketing is all about staying in front of people and being remembered.

CINDY Lisa makes a point — whether it is a brochure, postcard, rack card, or business card, having something with your information on it to hand out is imperative. How attractive it is will determine how productive it is.

Business Cards

SPIRITUAL BUSINESS TIP #49

You should always be about to run out of business cards.

CINDY If business is good, you should always be about to run out of business cards. Like brochures, online printing services make business cards for very low cost. Here, again, think about design. I recently made up new business cards and tried to put all my information on them, including a little graphic of my book, *Soul Soothers*.

It was so crowded that the print was almost too tiny to read. On top of that, I picked a dark background color that matched my book cover, but did not offer the right contrast for easy reading. Learn from my mistake: less is more with a business card. Use easy-to-read, decent-size fonts (at least 10 point) and, depending on your business, your name, company name, telephone, email, website, a *few* words as to what your business is, and if you have a business location, that too.

If you work out of your home, do not put that address on your business card. You don't want someone walking up to your house at 10 pm., uninvited. You can add things like your social networking address, online booking service, etc., if there is enough room. Or better yet, use the backside of your card for that information.

Again, remember, not crowded and easy to read is what will make your cards stand out. A graphic, appropriate for your business, or a picture of you is also nice, but is not worth it if it will crowd your card. Lisa hands out an Angel Message Card that shows simply an angel message, her name, and her website. People are less likely to throw out a card if it has an angel message on it, and anyone who wants to contact her can go to her website for that information. I sometimes put the Mercury Retrograde dates for the next year or two on the back of my business card. This dates your business card; so if you choose something like a calendar or other dates, don't make too many cards at one time.

LISA My angel prayer card was a stroke of angel insight. I'll tell you the story behind my angel prayer cards. A couple of years ago my cousin came down with cancer. Fortunately, it was caught relatively early, but of course because it was cancer we were all worried for him.

I did what I am inclined to do, which is to pray for the angels to help him heal and take care of him. The prayer that came out was channeled and guided by my angels and I was struck by how beautiful it was. Immediately, I was told by my angels to put the prayer on a card so he could keep it with him.

I went to my online printer to see if I could design one that I liked. They happened to have a perfect template and an angel image that I loved. It all happened so quickly and easily. I realized that I could give the card to others who might need the prayer. I was told to give the angel prayer card to those who asked for it as a gift and so I did.

On the back of the card is my website and that is all. I have had people from all over the world requesting the angel prayer card.

As Cindy says, and I agree, business cards are a must and there really is no reason not to have one. It is so easy to create business cards these days, especially with online print services. You can print 100 business cards for the cost of shipping. The templates that they use online are beautiful and professional.

You should always have a business card ready to give someone, whether you are out for personal reasons or for business. When you are an entrepreneur you are always promoting yourself and the best way to do that is to have a business card ready to hand someone when they ask what it is you do; they might become your next customer.

Keep your business card simple and only include the most important pieces of information because you don't have much real estate on a business card to print a lot of information. You should put your name and your contact information on the card. Include your business name as well unless you are "doing business as" your name. You can include your title. Here are some examples: Reiki Practitioner, Massage Therapist, Angel Reader, Naturopath, Energy Healer.

It is best to just pick one, or at most, three things, which should be the main aspects you want to promote yourself as. I promote myself as a Teacher, Author, and Speaker specializing in Intuition. This is on my website and all my promotional material.

You can also put down your phone number, physical address, website and email address. I am moving away from too much contact information such as my physical address because none of my work happens there and most people contact me online or over the phone.

I have seen the newer generation of cards only have a website address, which makes sense because all the contact information and more is there. There are still people though who do not have computers or access to one, so for them, at the very least include your name and phone number.

CINDY I just had a client who has no computer. As time goes by, not having a computer or at least Internet access will be less and less common. But for now, if your clients do not all have easy access to the Internet, for whatever the reason, include a phone number.

LISA I have a business logo, which I have registered as a trademark. You don't have to have a logo and if you do have a logo you do not have to trademark it. I like having a logo because I can put it on all my promotional material, websites, and social media or my products such as CDs, books, DVDs and apps. If you do have a logo you should put it on your business card.

PRESS KIT – YOUR MARKETING BLUEPRINT

LISA A press kit is a set of materials that includes information and items such as photos, a bio, and business description that others can use to promote you and your business. It's a nice package that you can put together to give media people but, if you so choose, you can also give to others so they can get the word out about your business more easily.

The value is when you have it all set up, it will be a consistent message you give to everyone. The wording and presentation will be the same whatever event or project you do.

For example, you may be performing your services at a local holistic center and they will promote you to their customers. You can give them the press kit so they have all the information and materials to use in their promotions.

This also goes for if you are going to be interviewed perhaps on the radio, on television, in a webcast, or other production that is shown to the public. Sometimes a press kit is referred to as a media kit. In the past, a press kit would be a hard copy of materials, though now it's most often in digital form, which is often preferred so others can more easily use it.

CINDY Press kits aren't only for famous celebrities; you will use elements from your press kit in all your marketing. Making up a press kit, either digital or hard copy, not only forces you to condense your information into a small, powerful presentation, it allows you to see the big-picture image you have created for you and your business.

Include in your press kit:

- Headshot – High resolution is a must.
- Personal Bio – Your credentials and what makes you special. Include three lengths; short, medium and long.
- Business Description – What your business is all about and its benefits.
- Featured Product or Service.
- Links – Links to blogs, websites, interviews, YouTube, etc. This works best in a digital press kit.
- Contact Information.
- Testimonials.
- Upcoming Big Events – Remember to keep this updated.
- Social Media Blurbs – Short promotional blurbs for people to use on their social networking pages.

Once you have your press kit together, you'll go back to it every time you need to do new marketing. It is one-stop shopping. Instead of going to ten different files on your computer, you just open your press kit and copy what you need!

Have someone else view your press kit and tell you what he or she thinks you are all about. Your values, your personality, your passion, your personal strengths, your business strengths, and your professionalism should all shine through in your press kit. Avoid clip art, but don't be afraid to sprinkle some pictures of you throughout.

Leave a lot of white space — a few powerful words are better than a long paragraph. This is where your fifty-word descriptions and one-sentence bullet lists are put to work. A press kit should be visually impressive. I use colors to create a sense of form as well as pictures and larger fonts. You can go to either of our websites to look at ours and get even more ideas.

Digital Press Kit

CINDY   This is the digital age, and even if your practice began 3,000 years ago, you want to stay as up to date in your image, marketing, and technology as you are in your technique.

Uses for a Digital Press Kit:

* To put on your website.
* To send out in emails.
* To include with press releases.
* To give out to prospective bloggers who might want to promote you.
* To have available for interviewers.
* To give to clients for parties, etc.

You never know when someone may want to write an article about you or when you might be asked to guest on a radio show. Having a press kit ready and available on your site goes a long way to having the prospective radio or TV show pick you over someone who does not.

It is also an excellent tool to send out when you get an inquiry from a customer. Often we use email instead of making a phone call, and a digital press kit is an easy inclusion in that email to give a prospective client, radio show host, or interviewer. I offer a digital press kit to clients who book psychic parties. They can then forward it on to friends rather than having me mail out my brochure.

The advantage of the digital press kit is that it is easily forwarded and it contains clickable links that allow your prospective client or interviewer to explore more detailed information about you. My husband and I do a lot of media events and it is so much easier to send one press kit that contains all the information the host needs.

When they are ready to market my event, they can easily download my high-resolution photo and use the write-up for my event, my bio, and any other information they may want. My husband and I also host speakers for a group we run and it is often a hassle to get the speaker's write-up, bio, and high-resolution picture. We wish everyone used a digital press kit!

LISA Digital photos are important for your headshots because it is the most convenient way to get a photograph to someone. Also it's cheaper than printing photographs and sending them by mail. Keep in mind that the photographs or pictures you have of yourself should be in high-resolution files, usually a JPEG file.

Many photographers these days will give you your photos in digital format as well as printed. Do NOT embed a photo into a Word document and send that as your photograph. These are less flexible to use. A high-resolution photograph can be used for print and online material. If necessary the high-resolution files can be reduced if need be, but a low-resolution photograph cannot be converted into a high-resolution one. High-resolution files can also be used for larger print projects, such as making an 8 x 10-inch printed photograph.

Another important thing to keep in mind is that all of your marketing material, whether it is in your press kit, on your website, or printed on paper should be consistent. You may change the wording to fit the page or size, but in general, it helps your brand to keep all the marketing phrases and descriptions the same. This also saves you the trouble of having to write something new each time.

By keeping your phrases and descriptions the same you are helping people remember who you are and what you do. It also minimizes confusion. Repetition helps people learn, and can help people learn and remember you.

Hard Copy Press Kit

CINDY The uses for the Hard Copy Press Kit are similar to the digital version, but sometimes your client requires a hard copy. Very infrequently, I am asked to send promotional material in the mail. Usually I just send my brochure, but sometimes the client needs more information. If you turn your digital press kit into a PDF using software like Adobe Acrobat, you can then print it out for mailing. All the information you need is in one place.

The only thing to remember is that you will need to turn the links into literal URL addresses that the person can input into his or her browser or take out that information altogether. Whether digital or hard copy, the following is what goes into a basic press kit.

Headshots

LISA   A headshot is not being shot in the head; it's just a photograph of mostly your face. Headshots are important to give you a professional image. Next to your website, a headshot is one of the most important things you need for your business if your business is to provide a personal service as opposed to a product. People want to see who they are getting the service from and you want to put your best front forward so to speak.

The best headshots are taken by a professional because they know how to frame you in the picture and literally put you in the best light. They also have the proper equipment to take a good photograph. Once you have a good professional photograph you can and will be using it in many places.

If you can't afford or find a professional, then here are some guidelines for a good headshot. The photograph should be a full front view of your entire face and your shoulders. Generally, you should not wear jewelry, though you can wear small earrings. Your clothes should be of a single color, without stripes or patterns. This will all bring the focus to your face.

You should be the only one in the picture. Make sure there is good lighting on your face so your features can be seen clearly. Here is a trick that my mother, who was an actress, gave me. When you smile and look into the camera, pretend that your best friend or someone you love is on the other side of the camera and smile as if you are looking at them.

Have a headshot that is color, not black and white because a color photo can always be made black and white digitally. If you have a photograph of yourself that you like but others are in the picture, I suggest you do not use it. Photos that are cropped to cut out other people look like photos that are cropped and it lacks a professional quality.

Once you have a headshot, make sure that you get a digital high-resolution copy of it, which should be 300 dpi (dots per inch ie., high-resolution). Once you have a digital copy of the photograph, you can use it many different places, such as on the web, in your online newsletter, in print for postcards, magazine ads, etc. A headshot should be part of your media kit, both hard copy and digitally.

CINDY   Headshots should be current. I have a tendency to change my hairstyle and my weight goes up and down. Mostly up these days, but you see my point. I used the same headshot for about 15 years. People would meet me and say, "*You don't look like your picture.*" Now that I know how easy it is to get a new headshot, I'll never postpone again. Although I must admit I haven't redone my sign with the short hair photo yet. That's on my to-do list before my next event. New signs are no longer the expensive investment they used to be. With printers such as Staples or Kinko's, you can get them done the same day for a very reasonable price.

LISA Cindy makes an important point about your photo looking the way you look today. One of the most common things I hear people say to me at public events is that they recognized me from my publicity photograph. Again, recognition of you and what you do is all part of building a business identity.

Bio

LISA A "Bio" is short for biography. It is a short synopsis of who you are, what it is you do, your background, and your relevant credentials generally in that order. It is also a quick way to introduce yourself either in written form or to be read by someone else. You should keep in mind it is also a way to indirectly promote yourself.

You want your bio to convince people that you are credible and that you have expertise in what you do. This goes a long way in motivating people to buy from you. I am amazed at how many professionals do not have a good bio. I have had many guests on my radio show who are well established in business and don't have a bio that is concise, easy to understand and read.

The first key to a good bio is how it is written. You should write it so it can be read easily and be understood. When you are interviewed the host will most likely just read your bio out loud. You want it to read so it sounds natural and not cumbersome. Remember brevity is very important. People have short attention spans. This will also force you to just put in your strongest points and leave out the weak ones.

Resist trying to include everything that you ever did, and instead, focus on what is the main Business Identity that we spoke about earlier. You can include what supports it. You can tell a story but make it short and to the point. If you are not good at writing you may want to seek help from someone who is.

CINDY Although I've always used third person, I like Lisa's suggestion to write a bio in first person. Anything that helps the prospective client to know you better is worth the effort. First person means you are telling it like it is, as if you were speaking directly to the person reading it.

I have recently changed my bio and much of my website to reflect this more personal "first person" approach. Here is an example of first person:

- "I have been a psychic for over 20 years. My most exciting project in 2013 was finishing my master's thesis."
- Third person reads as if someone else is speaking about you.
- "Cindy has been a psychic for over 20 years. Her most impressive project in 2013 was the completion of her master's thesis."

Third person can be a little less intimating and feels less ego-centered. Both first and third person have their place. As Lisa says, first person is great for a less formal or more intimate view into your life whereas third person is great for someone else to read, like a radio host or someone introducing your talk.

LISA   One of the most frequently used items in my press kit is my bio. Your bio will and can be used when you speak at a conference or event, when you are interviewed, when you create marketing material for your services, when you are performing your services at a public event, and so on.

The producers of events, such as holistic fairs or organizations that hold events, will ask for a bio from you so they can publish it on their websites or in their marketing materials. These bios are almost always requested to be a certain length by "word count" which is the number of words in the text of your bio.

Sometimes the length requirement is given in number of characters. For this reason, I have three standard bios that are of different lengths: small, medium and large. I then can modify them slightly for specific lengths of required word counts. My short bio is about 85 words and is under 150 characters, my medium length bio is about 150 words and my long bio is about 320 words.

All the bios are generally the same in what they say, and how they are written; the difference is that the longer ones have more detail.

Business Description

CINDY   In a business description you take all the work you did in Chapter 2, describing what type of spiritual business you are, with short write-ups and one-sentence bullets to tell people what your business is all about and the benefits they will receive from it.

For the best business description, keep it short and use a lot of white space. By white space, I mean blank space on the page. People tend to skim, so the less words, the more likely they will read it all. If you use headings, make sure they are descriptive and encourage the person to read further. "Massage Services" is pretty bland, but using something like "Relaxation Options," may find people more intrigued about what you do because it is offering a result they want!

Featured Product or Service

CINDY First you feature the main product or service that you want to offer. You may spend a little more time describing what it is and what the benefits are. Include a picture or two if that is relevant. For example, my first digital press kit was centered on my book *Soul Soothers*, so I had a page devoted to *Soul Soothers*, which included a short description and reviews. My psychic press kit presents my main psychic services along with a picture of me.

Additional Products or Services

CINDY It is likely that you have more than one product or service available, so you might have a page or a half-page devoted to your other specialties. Here you would use even shorter descriptions and include links to websites where people can get more information. I put my books, meditation CDs, numerology reports, crystal pouches and other products I offer in my 'psychic' press kit.

Links

CINDY Links only work in a digital press kit so it is necessary to type out the URL if you are using a hard copy press kit. Here is where you add links to your blogs, websites, interviews, video recordings, etc. Your links page should be organized, not just a bunch of links. Remember that if you are sending out a hard copy, you need to write out the actual URL address for links so a person can type the address into his or her browser.

Include social networking links and links to your blogs or wherever you have information about your business on the Internet. As your business grows, so will your list of links. I use Apple products, so I use the Notes feature to keep my links in one place. Anytime I get a new link, I add it to my "Link Note" and can then easily retrieve it for social networking, making new press kits, and sending to family.

LISA One of the unifying things I have done to make it easier for people to find various links and information related to me and my business is to try to put everything on my website. This way I only give out one link, which is my website: www.LMK88.com. I then have links on my website to my blogs, e-Store, membership site and to other things that I would like to refer people to on my website. It also makes it easier for others to remember where to go. My social media links are listed separately in my Press Kit as well as posted on my home page, but I only list the most popular ones, such as Facebook, Twitter and YouTube. Otherwise, all of my publicity materials just feature that one link to my website.

CINDY Lisa makes a good point here, you could simply put a link in your press kit to the Links page on your website. As she noted, it still makes sense to show links to your main social media.

Contact Information

LISA I personally like to keep it simple for people. I have found that it is easier for people to just go to the website to get my other contact information, *except* for those people who are non-computer folk, who need a phone number. The exception is on my business card where I put all of my contact information on. But any other time, like in an interview or online I always *only* give my website. This becomes a one-stop contact, plus they can sign up for my email list!

CINDY That is a really good point, Lisa. Whether it is simply a web address and phone number or if you choose to include more, clear accessible contact information is essential. It doesn't matter whether it is in your press kit, on your website, or on your brochure.

As discussed earlier, try to keep the length of your name and your website name short. Dave and I chose SpiritualSimplicityBooks.com for our books because SpiritualSimplicity.com was taken. We would have preferred the shorter name for two reasons: one it is easier to remember and two, it fits better on a brochure or business card!

Upcoming Big Events

CINDY If you are going to list upcoming events in your press kit, it is important to keep this section updated. If you have old information it will seem unprofessional, or worse, that you are no longer in business. I suggest you *only* put upcoming events in your press kit. Here you would list the date, time, cost, and a short description with bulleted points to show the benefits of attending. The same holds for a website — you never want old dates on a website.

Fancy promotional material may get clients to the door, but it is your professional, compassionate, and competent manner that will make them want to come back.

The next chapter is about how to stay professional and current so that you can always present your best for your business and your clients.

CHAPTER NINE

Staying Professional

• • • • • • • • • • • • • • •

KEEP UP TO DATE

SPIRITUAL BUSINESS TIP #50

It is important to keep up with the latest in your spiritual business field.

CINDY There is always a new kid in town who has an innovative technique or a new book that your clients have read and want to ask you about, so it is important to keep up to date with the latest in your spiritual business field. Here are some ideas of how to stay current.

Network with Other Practitioners

CINDY Creating a referral network of spiritual practitioners is not only a smart marketing tool; it keeps you up to date with new ideas and marketing opportunities. Also, your visibility will be increased by how much you are involved in the spiritual community. You can learn from other practitioners about what is new in your field, as well as exchange helpful marketing and business tips.

It is an ego-focused personality who believes he or she cannot learn from another person. I teach all sorts of metaphysical classes, but always learn something when taking another person's class. It could be how to handle a difficult student, something about the topic I never knew, or sometimes, what not to do in a class!

Taking others' classes also introduces you to more people. I would not recommend pursuing someone else's client, but you'll learn what type of people are drawn to other practitioners and why. Don't be afraid to ask people what they are getting out of the class or service or what they like most about it. Meeting and talking with other practitioners' clients is a winning tool for self-evaluation of your business.

Creating a referral network is a smart marketing tool and keeps you up to date.

Mastermind Groups

LISA   It's very hard to do things on your own; especially as a small spiritual business owner, you are often working in isolation. Mastermind groups are made up of peer practitioners who are willing and available to meet and give each other support and share ideas to help each other with their businesses.

The format of a mastermind group is each participant will be getting help from the rest of the group through brainstorming, providing advice and ideas to assist that individual in their business. Each participant will receive this assistance one by one in the course of the meeting.

The wonderful thing about mastermind groups is that you can receive insight for your business from an outside observer. This provides valuable perspectives on how to improve your business that you wouldn't be able to get on your own. Because the mastermind group is made up of other business owners like yourself, they know what you are going through.

They may be able to help because they have gone through the same issues or problems and solved them, or they're just there to help you figure some things out to improve your business. Because you meet on a regular basis the group can follow each other's progress.

The group could also provide motivation by holding you accountable for your self-appointed goals. I have found having an accountability partner really helps me accomplish more of my milestones and goals because I have someone there to root for me and celebrate with me in getting them done.

I am more motivated to make sure I reach those milestones, because I don't want to disappoint them or myself when we meet. If you can find a group of peers that you can get together to create a mastermind group with, it can be highly productive and help you make your business successful.

If you want to create your own mastermind group, keep in mind that a mastermind group is not a class, it is not for group coaching, and is not necessarily for networking, though networking is often a result. It is important that the mastermind participants are committed to helping each other.

The purpose of the group is to provide feedback and brainstorm new ideas for each participant's business. Again, setting up a format of accountability will help each person stay focused and be on track to accomplish goals.

The group does not have to be large; in fact you can have a mastermind group of just two people. You can meet on a weekly or monthly basis, or whatever frequency suits the group. Most mastermind groups that are already established will invite new members through an application process to determine if the applicant fits the personality of the group, the peer level and experience.

Commitment is important to a mastermind group. Your mastermind group becomes your business advisors. You may find joint venture partners in your mastermind group and be able to leverage each other's reach. Established mastermind groups often have a leader or facilitator who the group can learn from as well. To be part of an established mastermind group you usually have to pay a monthly fee to participate.

I have found that my mastermind partners are invaluable in helping me gain an outside perspective of the initiatives I'm putting in place for my business. Each time I begin a new marketing approach or offer a new product or service, gaining insight from these business owners who are of like mind is invaluable in giving me feedback, and then connecting me with resources and people who can help boost the productivity and effectiveness in my new business projects.

In a mastermind group there is no competition, just mutual support and benefit. If you are lucky enough to find one you can truly improve your business quickly. Members can cross promote each other's businesses. Connections can be made by extending your reach into other parts of your industry or related fields that can provide resources, or relationships that you couldn't find on your own. There is power in a group because they can work together and collaborate to achieve more.

CINDY Lisa, I have been part of a mastermind group for years and did not even know it! My friend Virginia Waldron and I have this type of support. We have lunch, which we consider a tax deduction, and brainstorm where we are going with our businesses and how to handle difficult work situations. She and I are support for each other and we hold each other to our goals. We do not have a formal time to meet; it is more on a need-by-need basis. Being friends is helpful because we can be truly honest with each other.

Attend other practitioners' events

SPIRITUAL BUSINESS TIP #52

A supportive spiritual community is one that will be viable for a long time.

CINDY One of the things I like best about our upstate New York spiritual community is that we support each other's events. I don't attend every class or meeting, but I try to get out to other practitioners' events, or better yet, co-sponsor those events. This is how you meet new people. The goal is not to steal someone's client but to enlarge your visibility and support the spiritual community.

A spiritual community that supports its members is one that will be viable for a long time. It is important to remember that the need for spiritual practitioners is growing and that there are enough clients to go around for everyone. Everyone is different, and your spiritual nature and uniqueness will be revealed at these events without you ever pulling out a business card.

BUSINESS DEVELOPMENT –
IMPROVE TO GIVE MORE

Learn More So Your Business Can Grow

LISA Don't be "too cool for school" in your business. Every business entrepreneur benefits from continuous learning and education. There are always new things you can learn to improve your business. The best step you took in this arena was to learn from reading this book!

You can expand your knowledge on your field of expertise and how to increase business performance. I am always learning and I've found that it allows me to try new things I've discovered that improve not just myself, but my business as well. For example, even though I'm very technical and have a degree in Electrical Engineering, I still am studying how today's businesses are using technology.

There are always new things being developed and, to me, it's actually exciting to find better, faster and easier ways to do things. I also continue to learn about topics that are related to my expertise on intuition, such as metaphysics, brain science, metaphysical energy and energy healing, etc. This helps me expand what I have to offer to my customers who are often interested in the same topics. An additional benefit of continuous learning is that you find out how others are succeeding. Learning about the winning solution someone else has made work for themselves can be helpful to you so you don't have to make mistakes finding out how to do the same thing. In terms of your business and synergizing with your existing customers, learning more will help you create more products and services for them to purchase, which keeps them coming back.

Many people just focus on one thing to offer or sell, and then when their customers buy it, there's no follow-on business. Continual expansion of your offerings and services is what will sustain your business and keep it growing. Remember, those who have bought from you are more likely to buy again. Don't loose that opportunity to serve them!

What to Learn and How

LISA   If you're not used to learning more or don't know where to start, here are some areas that could be helpful to you in expanding your business and helping yourself! You can take a class in topics that are related to your line of business.

For example, I actually pursued getting my PhD in metaphysical sciences for two purposes; one was because I wanted to learn more about metaphysics in a comprehensive way, but also because the degree would give me credibility. In any business you own, customers are looking to you to be the expert or the one who is knowledgeable. So the more knowledge you have, the better it is for your business.

Some of you might be required to take continuing education credits to maintain your license. Take the opportunity to learn things that can expand your business, and if you're able to, choose the kinds of classes your clients are looking for an expert in.

When I wanted to manifest growing my business, I asked for guidance from my angels and guides. I asked for more customers to come to me and that my client base grow exponentially. I wanted them to magically appear through manifesting them. But the messages I received told me that I needed to focus on marketing.

While I have a lot of experience and knowledge in sales and marketing, my messages told me I needed to gain new knowledge on how to market combining my technology background and my sales acumen. I knew I had to learn more, but that was okay with me because I love to discover new and better ways to do things. This is what learning is really all about, finding out new clues, new tools and better things you can do to make your business soar.

Learning about Internet Marketing and then implementing the techniques and infrastructure has expanded my reach, while boosting my following and customer growth tremendously. I am now passing that knowledge on to you.

CINDY I have never taken a class, no matter how basic it is, in which I haven't learned something. I sometimes take a class for teachers with the intention to learn different teaching skills, and I still pick up some tidbit about the subject that I hadn't known or had forgotten.

One thing I particularly suggest you continue to work on is your computer skills. With the way the world is going digital, and how quickly technology changes, your need for computer skills is continually evolving. As Lisa mentioned, you want to stay current in your field so you can continue to educate your clients.

This is important. I also feel strongly that learning for your own interests is vital. When I went back to school for my master's, everyone else was going to get their job to pay them more. I am self-employed and I wasn't giving myself a raise when I got my degree. I went to school because I had a yearning to learn more. I plan to use that knowledge writing a book on the mystics' journey to spiritual maturity, yet I went to school to quench my thirst for learning. I feel learning is always enriching, whether you can "use" the knowledge for your business or not. So I recommend that you learn for your clients and for yourself.

Find a Mentor

LISA Finding a mentor or "guru" who can help you in your business is the best way to accelerate the improvement of areas you may not be so good at or lack knowledge in. They say when the student is ready the teacher will appear.

I also ask spirit to help guide me to the right teacher or mentors. Don't expect to find *the* one and only teacher who can help teleport you to the highest level in every area of improvement that you want. I used to think that would be the ideal. I've come to realize that you can find specialists who can teach you expert knowledge in specific areas that you require. You can find someone to just teach you how to market yourself, or someone else who can show you how to organize your administrative tasks.

Even though I already had over 15 years of business, sales and marketing background, I knew I could always learn more, and as Cindy mentioned in the beginning of this chapter, staying up to date is critically important to any business. I knew that the best resources would come to me through guidance from the Universe.

Once I asked spirit for guidance and to send me mentors to help my business: they began to appear. Books came across my path written by "mentors" that were perfect for launching me into the next level of marketing, sales, copywriting, product creation, leveraging the Internet and even personal high performance.

People began to show up in my life who were experts in areas that I needed help in, some were already clients, some were friends, and some just appeared out of nowhere.

When I needed help in creating my online videos, a friend who just completed his master's in online media, specifically video, and had been producing his own videos, helped me get started in what equipment and software was best to buy to make my own videos.

A client who is a professional lighting expert for a national TV station helped me with learning about lighting and again buying and setting up my studio lighting. Another friend who is a phenomenal soft-sell sales person gave me pointers on how to build the right relationships to boost my business. I began to come across professional gurus whose major focus was to build a business exactly like mine as a speaker, teacher and author.

The fit was perfect so I took their classes. My knowledge expanded exponentially. I've accumulated all this knowledge, put it into practice and built my business so I can now share it with you.

A mentor can also be anyone who has been there, done that before you, and is where you'd like to be. As Tony Robbins says, "Success leaves clues." You can learn from others just by watching them, or if you know them and have a good relationship, you can ask for their help. In this case, it is best to make sure that if you do ask for help, that you offer something of benefit to them first.

Reciprocity is what makes these relationships work. We all have knowledge and experience that can be valuable to each other. The more we share the more support each other.

Read New Books

CINDY   I must admit, keeping up on new books is something I am not good at these days. For the last five years I have started and completed a master's program and written three books. Previously, I was an avid spiritual book reader. I find reading other authors' books forces my mind to look at new ideas and develop discernment.

Some of the information in the spiritual books I read is inspiring, but not all the concepts work for me. I had to develop a level of confidence and discernment that allowed me to take what I needed and leave what didn't work for me. I hope you use the same discernment when reading this book. Not everything an author writes is brilliant in any realm of literature, but almost every book has something you can learn from.

LISA I am infinitely curious and a perpetual student therefore I am always reading books, blogs, newsletters and eBooks. I love discovering new and better ways to do things, in both my business and my life. They say that no book written today has new ideas; they just rehash the old ones.

But this is okay because every author has a different perspective that can help you understand concepts in a way that someone else hasn't. Also, none of us have perfect memories, and we really do forget some of what we've learned in the past. Reading is a way you can refresh your memory and if you're reading a new book, it may have updated trends and information that you didn't know before.

If you're looking for books to read, the best thing to do is ask your mentors or teachers for recommendations. The other thing you can do is search on Amazon.com or online and see which books are popular or are written by an author you like. Not all celebrities and stars are good writers or teachers. People you may not know write gems so don't discount an author you are not familiar with.

I read a new book about once a month, and some highly motivated and accomplished business entrepreneurs encourage you to read one book a week! You don't need to read every book cover to cover, though reading a good portion of the book is better than just reading the first chapter.

If you've gotten this far in our book, I applaud you, since most people often just read the beginning of a book and that's it! Some books I do read cover to cover, others I read major chunks of the book that is relevant to what I need. I find time to read in the oddest places, and you may find you have more time to read than you realize.

With eBooks and eDoc readers like the Kindle where you can read a book on your computer, tablet or smart phone, you can read almost anywhere at anytime. You just need to remember to do it. I read while waiting for the doctor, waiting for the train, while I'm alone waiting on the grocery store line.

Sometimes at home, I can get the computer to dictate a book for me. There are tons of audio books out there now. You can listen to a book while you are driving or commuting to work. Most of the books I read are non-fiction for learning and these are easier to read in pieces than a novel.

Here are some suggested areas of topics that you may want to read for improving your business. You can search on these topics in Amazon.com and see what books come up that appeal to you. Many of these books you can now get on Kindle or as an eBook version:

- Small Business
- Incorporating
- Entrepreneur
- Marketing
- Sales Psychology
- Copywriting
- Building a platform
- Social Media Marketing

Know the Trends

CINDY Your clients, especially those who are beginning their spiritual journey, are most likely reading new books too. You'll need to know what information they are receiving so that you can talk to them about it and help them understand. Also, you don't want to become outdated. Vocabulary changes, ideas change. For example, when people in the 1960s were doing drugs to break through a limited mindset and reach higher states spiritually, drugs may have been necessary in some cases. But this is no longer true.

Now, we as a society have raised our vibrations higher than in the '60s and drugs take us to lower states of consciousness. That may be an extreme example, but spiritual practices change as the spiritual community evolves.

Reading current literature, including books and magazines, helps keep a pulse on your clientele's knowledge and gives you a heads up when trends are changing. If you are a massage therapist, for example, you may want to know if hot rock massages are out and Thai massage is in. The same is true for any business.

Take Classes

CINDY To make sure you stay current in your field, no matter what it is, usually means taking advanced classes. I often teach an advanced class in order to force myself to learn the subject matter, but I also take classes from others. One of the best classes I ever took was a half-day workshop on being a Medical Intuitive with John White in Lillydale, New York. I learned a lot in that short workshop.

LISA Classes and workshops may be a better form for you to learn in. Many people would rather take a class in person or have a teacher to follow than read a book. If you're the kind of person who needs to be guided actively to learn well, then a class is for you.

My business is mainly focused on teaching and many people have told me that they would rather take a class in person than do a class online. Then there are others who would love to take an online class because it can be done from the convenience of their home, or anywhere they have a device that connects to the Internet.

Many of my classes and workshops are taught both in-person and online, and students like both of them equally well. The material I have written for this book comes from both my in-person advanced class for those who want to become professional intuitive readers and my online class "How to Start Your Spiritual Business."

The students who take that particular in-person class enjoy connecting with other students and being able to see and hear me live. For my advanced class, students have told me they like networking with each other and they can begin to build their business relationships. If you like connecting with others, an in-person class may be for you.

Many of those students who have taken my online classes are often either really busy, don't have the time or money to travel or they live too far away to easily come to an in-person class. The students who took my online "How to Start Your Spiritual Business" class really like the ability to take the class whenever and wherever they are.

I also offered the students who took my advanced "Developing Your Intuition Level 2" class, access to the "How to Start Your Spiritual Business" online class for free, because the class material on building a business was the same in both. This kept them engaged and also was a nice bonus offer to them.

Many times, online classes will give you extras and bonuses as incentives. The online class was also a form of "class notes" for them and students find that feature of online classes is useful. Because online classes may be new to you, I will explain more in depth about how they work in the next section.

Online Classes and Membership Sites

LISA Online classes and membership sites are becoming more prevalent and a popular way to learn. You can probably find an online class on almost any topic. For example, I know of online classes on how to use medicinal herbs, how to grow your own micro garden, and how to develop your intuition ... okay, that one's mine! There are many out there and the list is growing. You will have a variety to choose from.

Online classes are accessed on the Internet usually through a web browser. The classes can consist of videos, online documents, audio recordings, or other presentation materials that you can access and possibly download. Some online classes are membership sites where you can sign up for a month-to-month fee to have access to the content on the site.

An online course that has a one-time fee is usually a set of modules or content that you have access to indefinitely. My online "Developing Your Intuition" course follows this model. These courses may have modules that you can access one week at a time, so that you can progress through the course a little at a time and not be overwhelmed.

The course teacher is usually available online through email, special Q&A webinars or tele-conference calls. Often there are forums or a comments section for students to post questions and share their thoughts with each other and the teacher.

When I hold my own Q&A coaching calls, I interact with students directly and can "hand-hold" each student through exercises and give them feedback that is priceless over learning alone. Also, in this way the student doesn't feel isolated.

I've taken quite a few online courses and really enjoy learning from them and the convenience of accessing the classes whenever and wherever I am. Many students from around the world participate and it adds breadth and variety to the interaction. Online classes are new and for some people an unknown, but can be a very powerful learning tool. In many ways online classes have advantages over in-person classes. I hope that this helps you feel more comfortable and perhaps even motivates you to take an online class.

CINDY I love the idea of being able to be anywhere and still participate in a class environment that provides the opportunity to ask questions and get feedback. So many of us are too busy with family, jobs, and home life to travel somewhere once a week for a class.

Online classes are a great solution and, I think, the way future education is moving. You will get more out of the class the more you participate, so if you are not comfortable with online postings, I urge you to give it a try. Or, if not, find a local class where you can connect with like-minded people to learn. There are plenty of classes available both online and in-person for those looking to grow spiritually both personally and professionally.

BE ETHICAL

SPIRITUAL BUSINESS TIP #53

If your goal is to open a spiritual business, then you must be ethical or it is not a spiritual business.

CINDY Ethics are key to any spiritual business. Ethics can be thought of as a group of principles that govern your behavior. In this case, basic spiritual principles that govern your business practice. If your goal is to open a spiritual business, then you must be ethical or it is not a spiritual business. As Lisa said early on in this book, it is your spiritual attitude that makes your business spiritual.

Sadly, some clients have a tendency to want their spiritual practitioner to tell them what to do, and there is also a tendency for clients to take spiritual guidance as the last word. Do not allow this. You don't want to take on the karma of your client.

Spiritual practitioners can make a number of common ethical missteps. Many can be avoided by simply asking your guides or higher self that anything you say or do be for the Highest and Most Loving Good of the client. Here are a few no-brainer examples of ethical rules for a psychic that you may think are too silly to mention, but I have seen practitioners break them:

- If a client wants to know about someone else, ask and intend that you receive only what the client can know about. Don't force it. Intend that any information you receive be okay, on a soul level, for the person you are asking about.
- Always speak for the best of all those concerned, not just the client.
- Take the time to be prepared, in the best shape psychically, for your session with the client.
- Don't use alcohol or drugs before a session or interaction.

Confidentiality

SPIRITUAL BUSINESS TIP #54

Your client or customer will expect confidentiality.

CINDY When running any type of spiritual business, your client or customer will expect that anything you discuss with them is confidential. You should not talk about your clients with other people. The rare reason you might do so is if you are seeking legal advice about the client, you have a mentor you discuss client issues with, or if someone intends harm to themself or others.

I sometimes will talk over a problem or look for better ways to handle a situation with a fellow professional. Even then, you can speak about a client's issue without breaking confidentiality. *You do not need to mention the client's name.* You will notice that any examples I use when writing this book give no hints of the identity of the person I am talking about. The information you share with your client and your relationship with him or her is a sacred trust.

Judgments

CINDY Another ethical issue I have come across, and struggled with in the beginning of my career, is dealing with a client whose lifestyle choices go against your own moral code. It is important to be able to get yourself and your opinions out of the way when offering readings or any type of counseling for another person. You must keep your morality out of your session as well as making sure you do not project your own issues onto the client.

For example, I have had an addictive personality for as long as I re-member. If you put an open box of cookies in front of me, those cookies will soon be gone. I need to use portion control. My client might not have the same issues. Thus I cannot assume that for him or her, an open box of cookies next to the TV will be a temptation. This may be a silly example.

Another example relates to my opinion that extramarital affairs don't work out well. That is my opinion. But I need to not project it into my reading if someone is having an affair. I need to look at the client's situation fresh, without bias. I have actually seen the rare case in which the married person left his or her spouse and in turn married my client to live happily ever after. It's rare, but it has happened. It is important not to project your opinions, beliefs, or fears onto your client.

Another important point is that your service might be great for one person and not for another. Spiritual work depends on resonance between the practitioner and the client. It is impossible to have a strong connection to everyone. This is another reason why it is good to have a referral network. Someone else might be perfect for the client you don't resonate with.

By referring this client, you will receive better 'word of mouth' comments then if you try to work with the client and it doesn't go well.

Shifting Energy

CINDY Similarly, when working with a client's energy it is important to keep a few ethics in mind. As a healer or even as a lightworker, shifting someone's energy has consequences that go far beyond the physical. As a person's energy shifts, it affects them mentally, emotionally, and physically. It also creates a shift in people who are close by.

I taught a class on Hermetic Philosophy, which teaches people how to shift their energy as well as the energy of those around them. There was much conversation about the ethics of using Hermetic Philosophy. My students were disturbed by the thought of shifting other people's energy without them knowing.

I agreed with my students and was relieved that they perceived the ethical issues regarding such a powerful tool. As a healer, you are being paid to shift your client's energy, yet that does not release you from doing so in an ethical manner. Here are some of the results of my students' conversation on the ethics of shifting energy:

- It is not your job or responsibility to shift someone else's energy. As a practitioner, your client is asking you to do so, which would be different.
- Inform the client of the full ramifications of their shifted energy, including, if you know it, the consciousness that must change in order to maintain the shift in energy.
- Ask that any time you shift energy, it is for the Highest and Most Loving Good of all those concerned.
- If you shift energy of others in a manipulative manner, you are really emulating the energy of manipulation, and that is the energy you will attract to yourself and client.
- Never *force* a shift of energy in another person or environment. Period.
- Shifting energy is best used on oneself rather than on others. It is a strong tool for spiritual growth that backfires when misused.

Many of us have a tendency to think that our energy is always wanted or needed. I feel this is not the case. The Soul knows if it needs to "take in" a gift of energy from another, so unless specifically asked by someone in a healing setting, I suggest you present your healing energy like a butler presents a silver platter.

Try leaving the energy you are sending outside the person's energy field so that if he or she is not able to process it now, you won't create an overload. You may not even know if the Soul chooses to accept or decline. If you are not sure the energy is accepted, you can continue to send it, but intend that if the energy is not accepted it remains outside the recipient's energy field in case it is wanted later.

Or you can ask that it return to the Light, its source, to be used for healing energy for someone or something else. It is important to remember that it is not our energy that a person accepts or declines. We are just the channels, not the source. Whoever receives this energy then needs to process it. He or she might not have the stamina to do so at that time.

The intended recipient might feel perfect the way he or she is or welcome the energy you offer and take every last drop. We can't really know if the person needs energy, and he or she consciously may not know. The Soul has the bigger picture; so offering any healing energy to the Soul without pushing it into the person's energy field, where it has to be dealt with, allows us to ensure that we are being respectful and helpful.

Helping Too Much

CINDY Helping too much is also a touchy subject in spiritual business circles. I will give you my take on it and leave you to make your own decision. As spiritual beings, we feel good about helping others. We are taught that service is the best way we can give back. There is truth in this, but we must make sure we don't take away someone else's Karmic lessons.

If Karma is to create balance for a soul's evolutionary growth, and we create an environment where he or she is not held responsible for choices made or actions taken, we could be delaying that soul's growth. That is just my opinion. Here is an example:

An ex-boyfriend of mine had issues with his temper. Though he had never taken it out on me, it usually came out when he was frustrated. He was trying to bring more spirituality into his life, but his frustrations and temper sometimes got the best of him. He got frustrated one day and punched a time clock. He hurt his hand pretty badly. I had just come home from healing school where I had learned how to fix things like that. I felt so good that I could take the pain away and so I did. With his pain gone, he pretty much forgot about the situation and the frustration/anger issue he could have been looking at. I am sure he had to deal with his frustration and anger again, and I hope it didn't hurt as much the next time.

What was my role in this incident? If I hadn't made the hurt go away, he might — I stress the word *might* — have looked at how destructive his temper tantrum was and experienced some growth. I put my "need to show I can do it and also to feel good about myself" in front of what was truly best for him. By taking away his pain, I thought I knew what he needed, but in hindsight, I think I was wrong.

The point is to balance your need to help, and your preconceived notions of what service is, with learning when helping is a healthy loving thing to do and when it is a co-dependent reaction.

Work to understand why you are helping. Did the person ask for help? Did you ask the person if they wanted help? I don't think there is a cut-and-dried answer for this situation; it's just something to ponder the next time you get the urge to help.

Psychic Sharing When Not Asked

CINDY   I can't tell you how many distressed clients have called me because someone walked up to them in a grocery line or hair salon and said, "*I have a psychic message for you...*" or "*I have a feeling...*"

Well-intentioned or not, it is not ethical, kind, or helpful to share when not asked. It usually freaks out the receiver of the information more than it helps. I think you should keep your intuitively received messages to yourself unless asked, but if you feel you have no way to hold it in, tell the person what you do for a living and that you have a feeling about her you would like to share.

Tell her it is not dire — and if it is, go back to Rule #1 and keep your mouth shut. Hand the person a business card and tell her that if she wants to call you, you will give her the message, no charge. Then it is up to the person if she wants to hear it or not. The session must be free of charge, otherwise that is hooking, which is very, very unethical.

Actually, the best thing to do if you have a message for someone is to ask Spirit to find a better way to deliver it. Ask that the person receive the message in a way that is for their highest and most loving good, without having to come from a stranger on the street. I have dealt with enough nervous clients to know that you may think you are doing a good deed, but it is rarely received as such.

LISA   Students ask me quite frequently whether they should share a message they receive for a stranger. First, I tell them that if they are just beginning to develop their skills the answer is a definite no. You wouldn't want to have the medical student you just met at a party offer to give you a medical treatment right then and there, would you?

As a beginner definitely keep your messages to yourself. Even if you feel they are messages that are urgent or need to get to the person. With your fledgling skills you may be right or you may not be. The Universe will find another way to get the message through to them without you.

If you are more advanced in your skills, you may have a bit more discernment in a clear and true message, but ethically, it's probably not a good idea to just share. Cindy gives a great suggestion on how to share if you feel you must.

Just be aware that you don't know how a stranger may react to your message, and the reaction may not be pleasant if you just blurt out your message to them. This brings up an important point about Ego, which we'll cover next.

Ego

LISA As a spiritual business owner you'll want to keep your Ego out of your business. Yet, your Ego is needed to be able to put yourself out there as an entrepreneur who is selling your services. At the same time, if your Ego takes over and gets too big, you'll energetically push clients and customers away because spiritually they'll sense your offerings may not be coming from your heart.

As a spiritual practitioner you come to understand that, as you grow spiritually, you are the channel for the higher spiritual energy to work through. It is when you start to think *you* are the great healer, or the great psychic, or the great teacher, that ego comes into your work and spirituality runs out the door.

This is particularly an issue for an intuitive reader, angel reader, psychic, medium, etc. As Cindy mentioned, and I have also found, being the one who connects and brings messages from Divine and Spirit sources causes people to hold your messages in high regard. It is a huge responsibility to bring messages to people.

Putting the skeptics aside, those who come to you for a reading because they trust you will bring them true messages, will expect you to let them know when you are giving them a message and that it's not coming from your opinions. I have found that the messages I give are weighted so heavily that people will take them as directives from God.

You need to remember you are only the messenger. You are not infallible when interpreting messages and that you must explain when you are giving your own opinion and when you are giving a message.

As an angel reader, I explain in the very beginning of a reading that I am just the messenger. That I pass on messages from their angels, and angels will never take away anyone's free will. Therefore, the messages are for guidance only. Everyone needs to be responsible for his or her own actions.

As practitioners we also do not want to, and should not, take on the responsibility of someone else's life. For example, I explain that angel readings are life guidance and not for deciding whether or not a person should buy this brand or that brand of car. This also gets my Ego out of the way, I am just the angel messenger, and therefore, I am not giving my opinion or judgment about someone.

The first thing you must do as a reader is to put your Ego aside. I have a disclaimer page on my website that explicitly states that everyone who comes for a reading is responsible for his or her own actions and decisions. I also have a set of pages on my website explaining what an angel reading is and answer frequently asked questions. As a practitioner, if you follow similar tenets, then you must follow them.

Although my intuitive readings are mainly as an angel reader, I also offer Mediumship, which is connecting to past loved ones. I do this because many people who come to me for a reading are seeking messages from those they love who are no longer with us. I have studied how to do Mediumship and have become quite good at it.

Seeing how other students have reacted to their own Mediumship abilities by becoming too impressed with themselves and their readings was a sad example of how the Ego can corrupt a spiritually based service. Over and over I would hear them regale us with stories of their "amazing" readings and hits.

Even as a teacher of intuition and psychic development I hear these stories told with such pride expecting others to be in awe. I love to hear intuition and psychic stories, but not like that. Too much Ego can take you away from spirituality; you can fall into the trap of competition and wanting to be better than others.

These budding Mediums become enamored with their newly found "gift" and the strong emotions elicited in sitters who come to their readings. They begin to believe that this ability has made them special and important. They forget that they are only the messengers, not the message. They also forget that everyone has this ability, that they are neither different nor special from others.

Students in my Developing Your Intuition Level Two class learn how to do Evidential Mediumship, which is a powerful way of demonstrating a connection to deceased loved ones. I leave Mediumship for the end of the course because it can be nerve wracking for people when they have to perform and give messages that can be validated or not.

When messages are validated it is a huge Ego booster, if they are not validated, it can be very demoralizing. Mediumship can bring out the competition between people, so I urge everyone to keep their Ego in check whether they receive validation or not.

Fortunately, every one of my Level Two students was able to receive amazing evidence and messages from their sitter's deceased loved ones. The basis for Mediumship skills is intuition, which we all have, so whether you are highly intuitive, a great Medium, or an amazing healer there is no reason to feel that you are better or superior to anyone else.

CINDY Lisa is good at Mediumship and feels comfortable saying as such. I am a good Psychic and I have no issues marketing the fact that I am skilled. Saying you are good is not Ego. Ego is thinking you are better than everyone else, you are infallible, or that you are the one who has the wisdom.

Accuracy and Free Will

CINDY I have had clients come to me upset because they were told something negative by a psychic and felt they had no ability to change it. I tell my clients that what a psychic or other intuitive professional sees about the future may be the most likely way a situation will play out, but that is not written in stone and it is definitely not guaranteed to happen just because a psychic sees it happening.

We all possess free will and thus we can change almost any future predicted event unless it is some big destiny event, which is rare. If you see something in the future that might be scary for the client, talk to them about free will and how they can change their future. Empower them to make changes to create a more positive tomorrow.

This not only applies to the intuitive arts. I had a client come back from a spiritual health care practitioner who scared or pressured her into buying more supplements than necessary. It is important to empower your customers or clients into making important decisions with your advice but without forcing them to accept your truth as their own. Let them know what they can do to heal or help themselves. Give them options and the space necessary to allow them to choose the action they feel is right for them.

I have also heard of psychics or other spiritual practitioners who insist they are guaranteed to be absolutely correct. *This is nonsense.* No intuitive information is 100 percent accurate. Many practitioners may disagree with me, but I feel predicting accidents, death, etc., can be harmful, because you can be wrong and you can create panic within your client.

However, if your information can keep the client from a dire situation, then find a tactful and responsible way to tell her about what you see. Remember, you can be wrong or be receiving a non-literal message. Here are some ethical tips about accuracy:

- Don't keep asking the same question over and over again looking for a different answer.
- Trust your guidance, but know you can be wrong.
- Offer the client the opportunity to ask questions.
- Discuss free will with your client.
- If you are not sure if you should say something … *Don't.*
- Remember, we are only as accurate as our channel is clear and our clarity can vary from day to day, hour to hour.
- If you are selling a product, inform the customer about the pros and cons of it and then let him or her decide what to buy.

I think you get the point, but accuracy is something I feel strongly about and an issue that comes up more than you would think. Whether you are a psychic, nutritionist, or teacher, you can be wrong, and probably will be a number of times. This doesn't mean you are bad at what you do; it means that you are human.

It is almost impossible for the channel of any type of information not to introduce his or her bias at some point. As a psychic, I tell people everything I see. But I have asked Spirit not to show me death, car accidents, etc. A psychic once told me I was going to have a car accident. I began driving around, paranoid and overcautious. I am sure I almost caused a number of accidents. It was very stressful for me. Then, coming out of a friend's house, I saw that someone had backed into my car. Yes,

I had a car accident. No… the stress I experienced was not worth the foresight.

When I just started my psychic business, I had a client with a very sick mother. He asked me how long his mother would live. I hadn't asked yet not to be shown such things, so I told him I thought she would live another three months or so. About two months later, the client came back furious. His mother had passed sooner than I said and he felt it was my fault that he couldn't say all he needed to say to her because I told him he had more time left.

This is the perfect example of (1) we can be wrong; and (2) predicting death is not helpful. This man was devastated because he believed that psychic information would be 100 percent accurate and I had not advised him otherwise.

I wish I had told him that timing in the psychic world is not exact and that I had empowered him to tell his mother everything he needed to right away. This brings me to my last point on ethics.

Empowering Your Client

CINDY   The best clients are those you have empowered to the point that they no longer need you. These clients become advertising success stories, demonstrating your ability to empower clients to a point where they can succeed in whatever issue they came to you with.

The best advertising is "firsthand," in the form of a testimonial or word of mouth. So remember to ask for testimonials or feedback. We create a success story for our spiritual business by empowering our clients and avoiding dependency. When I first started, I had a client who kept calling about the littlest of things.

When she called to see if she should re-string her tennis racket, I realized I had created a dependency issue. She had given her power over to me to make all her decisions. This was a very unhealthy situation and a huge lesson. I had to explain my concern and limit her sessions to once a month. She ended up not calling at all, and I assume she went to someone else to whom she could hand over her personal power.

It is better to have the client leave than for you to be part of creating an unhealthy situation. I have had to speak to clients about this only a few times, but thankfully, I usually see the situation happening before it gets extreme and we usually can continue working together without the dysfunction.

Walk Your Talk

CINDY One of the best ways to be of service in an ethical manner is through "walking your talk." By this I mean we empower others by being a positive example of what a person on the spiritual journey looks like. It is not expected that you be perfect — that is not what a person on the spiritual journey looks like. Trust that through seeing how you live your life, those around you see what spiritual growth looks like in another person and can recognize the positive results.

When we create an "openness of being" — in other words, an outward attitude that allows others to ask us questions — we know that if they have questions about the spiritual life, they will ask. When we have their free will attention and permission, then we can start to share our wisdom.

Finally, as a spiritual practitioner, it is not your job to tell someone else what to do. You are there to empower, and if asked, offer insight so that your client can decide, on his or her own, the best path to follow.

With that said, we feel the best path to follow is one that brings you into balance. The final chapter is designed to help you balance your new business, family, and life in a way that allows you to be the best you can be in all areas of your life.

CHAPTER TEN

Managing Family, Friends, and Your Identity

· · · · · · · · · · · · · · ·

FAMILY AND FRIENDS

SPIRITUAL BUSINESS TIP #55

The more your family can see you being practical as well as spiritual, the less they will worry about you.

CINDY   You may find yourself having to figure out the best way to tell friends and family that you have chosen to open a spiritual business. Even studying spiritual topics can create an awkward dinner conversation.

Not all family and friends are comfortable with having a psychic or intuition development teacher around. If you are a life coach, your friends might be afraid you are going to try to change them. I remember giving a deposition for a case left over from my real estate days and the lawyer was extremely nervous that I might read his mind.

I don't read minds, and if I did, I doubt I would have wanted to rummage around in his. Yet he is a good example of the misinformation that abounds about the spiritual world and those who have chosen to be of service through it.

What I have found is this: the more you respect yourself, are comfortable with who you are, and are comfortable with the choices you are making, the more your friends and family will see you being practical as well as spiritual, and the less they will worry about you becoming the "crazy sister," or that you are going to hell.

This is not to say that they will be excited for you or every family member will react with joy when you talk about the journey you are undertaking. You will know your family issues better than Lisa or me. But most family members want to know that you are still able to pay your rent, that you haven't run off to follow some crazy person, and that you are happy. This is another reason why I recommend that you don't quit your day job until your business is self-supporting and making a profit. Your family and friends need to know you are going to be okay in the long run.

I suggest that you show friends and family who you are, long before you tell them about your business idea. Show them that you are being responsible, that you are becoming more patient, more loving, more forgiving, and all of the other good attributes a spiritual journey blesses you with.

Once they can see the change in you, you may find that they ask you what has changed. You can tell them about a realization you had, or a class that you took, that helped you become a more spiritual person. Let them sit with that for a while. I can almost guarantee, as they see more changes, that they will ask more about your transformation. Then you can share your hopes and dreams of running your own spiritual business and how you want to be of service by using the talents you've developed.

Remember, it isn't necessary that they take the spiritual journey with you, just that they don't interfere with yours. It also isn't necessary that everyone you know be supportive of your enterprise in order for you to launch your spiritual business.

If your family and friends already know you are on the spiritual path, then show them you have thought your business through. Show them that you have already saved enough money for the first and last month's rent along with the security deposit. Show them the marketing work you did (see Chapter 2) and how you plan to turn that material into the first steps of your marketing. Show them you are being responsible.

Tell them you are not quitting the day job until your business can support itself, or that you have already saved up enough to support you for the first year, so your business has the time to develop a strong financial foundation.

All this will help your friends and family not to worry about you. They will know your spiritual business isn't based on a wish or a hope, rather that you have a strong business plan for success.

LISA My difficulty was not with my family but with my friends since I have many circles of friends that range from those in my spiritual business, at church, my son's school, the community I live in, to many others. Certainly, depending on the group of friends, they may react differently to the kind of business I have.

I change my terminology based on whom I'm speaking with. I choose which parts of my work to tell people about. If they are friends who I know aren't familiar with the lines of business that I'm in or perhaps don't believe in metaphysics, I'll start with a general explanation.

For example, I'll say I am an author and a teacher and then some leave it at that, or it may lead to the question, "Oh, what do you teach/write about?" and then I'll tell them that I write on self-help topics. If they seem open and interested, I may say that I teach about how to connect with your inner guidance and how to develop your intuition. Some people are actually quite receptive and interested. You can use this model also for strangers.

HOW DO I EXPLAIN WHAT I DO TO STRANGERS?

SPIRITUAL BUSINESS TIP #56

Often people ask what you do for a living to be polite, so start with a mainstream-sounding explanation.

CINDY So, you have met someone on a plane and he asks you what you do for a living. How do you respond? Remember, in Chapter 2, you made up a few short answers for that! But before you speak, try this first.

When people ask what you do for a living, be polite. They really don't want to know too much. Start with something that sounds mainstream. For me, instead of saying I am a psychic, I say I am a counselor. Most people leave it at that. If they ask me more or I feel they are particularly interested, I tell them that I use my intuition to help people when they are in crisis or not sure what direction to take.

If someone knows what a psychic is, they will figure out I am a psychic. If not, then they can ask more if they choose or leave it at that. If you see the person's eyes dilate or they make a face, then back up to the last explanation and change the subject. They are strangers, their judgment is their own, and you don't need to be offended. However, I find most people are interested in the spiritual world and you can have a great conversation. Who knows, maybe you'll find a new client! It has worked that way for me.

BALANCING LIFE, FAMILY AND WORK

Life in General

LISA Just having a life is a full-time job, then add working into that mix and you really have a busy life. Add on a family and a part-time small business then time and life balance becomes very difficult. The first thing to realize is that you cannot do everything at the maximum level of productivity that you could if you only did one or two things alone.

Prioritizing is of utmost importance, and then time management. If you are not good at prioritizing then juggling many different things at once will be difficult. Just know that it's okay to get help from people who have specialized skills who can give you assistance in areas that perhaps you don't have to do yourself. If you are not terribly good at bookkeeping, you may want to get someone to help you or hire a service to give you assistance.

You can now get lots of freelancers to help you with many kinds of skills such as copywriters, graphic artists, web designers, virtual administrative assistants and even accountants. Many freelancers work virtually, online, so you now have a much larger pool of candidates to choose from and try the best fit. There are quite a few resources online that provide freelance services inexpensively.

One source, called Fiverr.com, connects freelancers with customers to offer them services for five dollars. Services range from creating a logo to building a website. Many online freelance service providers connect customers like you to a wide range of freelancers where you can post a job description for what you are looking for and then freelancers bid on your job. You can then elect which one to award your job to.

Have you ever felt that you don't get your projects completed? Many times the reason is because you're seeking perfection. Perfection never comes, because nothing is perfect. This is especially true for creating a new business on your own, because you have the freedom to make it the way you want and there are no outside deadlines.

So life balance becomes very important. One thing often suffers for another and then you may get frustrated. If you can move all the pieces along at a steady pace, with the knowledge that each step may not be 100% to your satisfaction but perhaps 80%, you'll get a lot accomplished.

I used to think that you could have everything and all could be managed through hard work and perseverance. Having a full life with a successful career, a family and kids, vacation time, time for work, leisure activities, taking care of home, and running a business could all be accomplished. After all, it seemed like other people were able to do it.

But I guess we don't always see what's behind the scenes. Even without a family all of these things are hard to accomplish; where all areas get the most of your attention, the most of your efforts, and be successful to your 100% satisfaction. So the best thing to do is to accept that not everything is going to be completed or accomplished at 100%. You might have to accept 80% and by doing that you may find that you accomplish more.

Time management gets even harder when we have a family, though some of the suggestions for families can apply to people who don't have kids or a spouse.

Family, Grandparents and Kids

LISA When you first get married, life becomes a little bit easier because, as my Dad used to say, two can live cheaper than one and you both are there to help each other with day-to-day tasks. Once you have a child, time management becomes much more complicated.

"Cheaper" now becomes more expensive with additional family members who are dependent. Time and resources become scarce when you are part of the "sandwich generation" that needs to take care of both children and aging parents. It is critical to be able to manage time, work and life, and stay balanced both emotionally and physically, so you can accomplish what is necessary and be productive in your business.

Getting help in general is a way to leverage your time and money so you can get more done and move your business forward. Help doesn't always have to be in the form of hiring people. If you are the kind of driven personality that most small business owners are, you probably tend to take on everything that you feel needs to be done.

It's important to know that it is okay to ask other people for help, particularly from your family. If you are the mom who is cooking and cleaning, holding a full-time job, taking care of the kids, and trying to start your business, you will quickly find yourself overwhelmed.

If you are a dad working long hours, and the handyman around the house and the guy who takes the kids to their afterschool sports practice or helps with their homework, and trying to start a small business, you too are going to find yourself overwhelmed and may not be able to accomplish what you want.

Either of you may want to think about getting outside help on a regular basis. For example you may want to get help cleaning the house or to hire a handy man or contractor to do those jobs around the home. It may be worth spending the extra bucks to free up your time, and to not have the worry of things not getting done.

You may also get your children to help with "chores" around the house. Some cultures have kids taking care of smaller tasks or even taking care of themselves and helping out the family with tasks such as folding the laundry, taking out the garbage or recycling, feeding the pets, or taking the dog for a walk.

It may take a little time to teach them at first, but once you've taught them, they now have a skill for life that not only teaches them how to take care of themselves, but also gives them real life experience.

We had my son start to learn how to fold his laundry when he was seven years old. Though he didn't start out as an expert, just learning this task early taught him how to be neat and organized. At first he didn't really like doing it, but after a while he got used to it. Now, 17, he prefers his laundry clean and neat; he even irons his laundry on his own!

CINDY Yes, it takes a while to show someone else how to do what you do, and it is likely that whoever you hire will not do it as well as you could if you had the time. That is the issue, though, isn't it?

Most spiritual practitioners don't have enough hours in the day. It's important to acknowledge that some chores are okay at 80% of perfect. I am sure Lisa's son wasn't that great at folding his own laundry at first. It is important to determine where your time and energy are best used.

For example, I only send out client birthday cards when I have someone who can do it for me. My helper moved and so I haven't sent out birthday cards in a while, which isn't exactly what I want, but my time is better spent on writing right now. I'll have to drop something I like doing until I find someone else to help me because my docket is too full.

It takes effort to find someone, but if you can get someone to help reduce your workload, it is worth the time to find and train the person. You may never find someone to clean your house as well as you do, but spending your time balancing your books or creating new ad copy might well be a better use of your time.

Think about hiring help the same way you do about marketing. How many clients or customers do you need in order to pay for the service? If it costs $80 to hire someone for three hours of cleaning, and your typical client spends $75 for a half hour of your time, then why spend three hours of your time cleaning? Your time is better spent marketing to attract that one client or actually working in your business.

Also, you may find that you need help only sporadically. Consider hiring a young person looking for occasional work. The girl who did my birthday cards got paid about $20, once a month. It took her about two hours to do the mailing. It was a win-win for us both. She had a little extra spending money and I only needed one client every other month to pay for her services.

LISA In life, we often have a mini-crisis that pops up here or there. Especially for the "sandwich" generation, which I am a part of, taking care of young children and elderly parents at the same time always brings the unexpected. It may be a sudden illness or injury. It may not be a physical crisis; it could be your kid with a problem at school or your parents having problems handling personal affairs.

As I write this chapter, I am going through a mini-crisis at home. My Mom is 87 and my Dad is 94 and has dementia. My mother is fully mentally capable of taking care of herself and Dad, and insists on doing so herself. Until recently, when she fell down a short flight of stairs due to being slightly dizzy from the flu. She broke her sacrum and was admitted to the hospital and then rehab for many weeks.

Suddenly, Dad had to stay with me and he requires 24-hour care. I needed to get help, and so I did. The first order of business in any crisis is to get help. When you do have a crisis you shouldn't be afraid to ask for help from other family members, friends, or outside services.

Nannies, baby sitters, and the college kid next door can be great resources and there are more and more professional services available for both children and the elderly. Your employer's human resources group may have a life-work counselor or services that can give you assistance in finding the help you need. The key thing is not to be afraid to ask!

The Day Job

CINDY I have been lucky in that I have not had a day job in a long time, yet I wear many hats and being an author, teacher, psychic, and coach tends to pull me in many directions. Lisa and I spoke earlier about breaking your time into chucks, in a way that allows you to work on multiple projects and I think this applies as well to the day job issue.

You need a stable income to be able to do your spiritual work, so you don't want to become a lackluster employee. If you are lucky to have a flexible job, with flexible hours, then you might think that figuring how to divide your energy and attention is simply a matter of maths. How much can you earn by working one job versus the other. Except that you have to take into account the potential for future income.

Let's say you have an event in which you are speaking at an expo or library. You don't have any income coming directly from that event, but you might get some clients from it. It would be shortsighted to ignore that opportunity. Even if you lose a few hours pay from your day job, it might make sense to do the event because of the potential of future clients. The important thing is not to jeopardize your day job. Often these events, and even clients, can be scheduled after work hours or on days you don't work.

LISA Having a day job to make a living, or a career that you are currently in but want to change, complicates balancing your time available for building your new spiritual business. I always tell people not to quit their day job until they have enough flow of customers, reach and income in their spiritual business, to not only cover the business expenses but also pay them an income.

It is a tough decision to make as to when you quit your day job. You will have to decide the best time for that based on how much reliable income you are making in your spiritual business.

You will need a steady flow of income that can cover your personal expenses and give you enough to make a living on. Keep in mind that in owning your own business, you are susceptible to the highs and lows in owning a business and your personal income can be affected.

Also, like life, your business may need an injection of extra cash to either grow or cover unforeseen costs. Careful consideration of both current and future monetary needs is important. Remember that you will need a pipeline of customers as well as constantly attracting new customers to make a business thrive and maintain income flow.

CINDY Your business income will cycle. Not only with the seasons, your income will also fluctuate with your energy, outside life influences, and the economy in general. When we had the economic crisis in 2008, my income dropped about 10%. That may not seem like much, but for me it was enough to create a pinch until I could reevaluate my spending.

Also, I find that if I am not feeling well, am upset, or if my life is hectic, I don't get as many clients. It is like the Universe is telling me to focus on my own needs instead of being of service to others. It is also a fact that when your attention is on your own issues, it is hard to be at your best for your clients.

It isn't always an issue around you that causes your business to slow down. When my husband was going through Stage 4 lung cancer, my business dropped significantly. The same happened when my mother was very ill. What if you broke a bone, do you pay yourself disability? Do you give yourself paid vacations? If I don't work, I don't make money.

We can't always plan for drops in cash flow, which is why it is important to have outside income until your business can afford to go without for a while. This is why I recommended having the "Oh No!" fund.

Keeping Home Time Sacred

CINDY Whether you work and live in the same location or simply spend a lot of time working on your business from home, it is important to have a sacred space for work. Yes, it might be easier to work in front of the TV or at the dining room table, and I do that, but you must keep a workspace that is as separate as possible, preferably with a door that you can close when your workday is done.

Why? You want to be able to leave your work behind so you can spend quality family or home time without having to look or think about all that still needs to be done. No matter how good your time management skills are, or how much help you get, there will always be projects unfinished and things to be done.

Being in your office is also a signal to your loved ones that you are working. Somehow it is easier for a family member to interrupt you when you're working from home. There is no way to totally eliminate the blurred lines between work and home, but having a designated workspace with a door is a big help.

Another potential disturbance to your sacred home time is the "office" phone ringing at all hours of the day and night. For the most part, I only pick up business calls from around 10 a.m. to about 8 p.m. I also don't answer during dinner, on holidays, and when I have company. I let the machine pick up. At least that is my intention, sometimes I don't realize how late it is and pick up at 10 at night and the person on the line is usually embarrassed, thinking he or she would get my machine!

I am never available for a session if someone calls me out of the blue. I am happy to schedule an appointment, but if the person is freaking out, I actually make him or her wait longer. No one gets a good reading when too upset, so this gives the client time to calm down.

Plus, it is a way I set personal boundaries. A client usually can expect it to take 24 hours minimum to get an appointment. Again, no rule is set in stone. If I have a good, steady client, one who is not too emotional for a reading, and I have the time, I might schedule something later that day; but never right then. You will find the personal boundaries that work best for you. After over twenty years in the business, I have come to really appreciate my downtime and I find the more I honor my time, the better psychic I am. My guides once told me, "Taking care of yourself is not selfish… it's essential!"

LISA Having your own working space is important, as Cindy says, plus if you are planning to take a tax deduction from using your home office it is necessary that you separate what you use for your business from your personal things.

Talk to a tax accountant regarding what you can deduct and what you need to do to keep your business items separate from your personal ones. If you are working from your home, a separate room or space is necessary particularly if you see clients in your home.

Even if you are working on the phone, you want to have a business space that focuses only on business. If a client or customer can hear your dogs barking or your children screaming in the background of your phone call, it will not make a very good professional impression.

The same goes for your home; if you are seeing a client at your home, it would be best to have a separate room or space where your personal life and home activity does not interfere when you are conducting business. Part of this is for your own sanity and mental separation of personal and work life, but also to maintain a professional image.

If you have a separate space or room you can work in, as Cindy says, a door is essential. I am fortunate enough to have my own home office, for which I had a door installed when we bought our house to keep out the noise.

I also have a separate meditation room where I meet clients and there too I can close the door. This separate space allows both you and your customer to focus, concentrate, and be in the energy and space of your work. As Cindy says, having boundaries is important, especially with how and when you are available. You may want to set "working" hours for yourself that you follow and let customers know when you are working and when you are not.

My business voice mail message says that, if you call on the weekend or holiday, I will return your call the next business day. I also don't pick up the phone after 5:30 p.m., because I have established that time as my cutoff for taking business phone calls. Once you establish your business hours, stick to them and let customers know what they are. Post the hours when you are available, and how to reach you, on your website.

Part of this is time management, which is key for a new business owner. Remember, you may be so excited to get your first customers that you want to bend over backwards to accommodate them, but they will understand if you say you are available only during certain hours. If they don't, then expect that they never will and you may not want them as future customers. It is up to you to decide when to make exceptions.

Cleansing My Space and Myself

CINDY Whether you work in a spiritual business or not, energetically we bring our work home with us. When working with people's physical, emotional, and mental well-being, as a practitioner or, say, a health food store owner, we are especially subjected to the energy of our clientele.

Think of chocolate chip cookies baking in the house. You can smell the cookies even before you get to the kitchen. If you take those freshly baked cookies to the office, you'll still sense the yummy smell of those cookies.

People's energy works similarly; it wafts outwardly and is psychically picked up. Those cookies could be eaten up right away and the house would still smell of fresh baked cookies! The same is true for energy. Even though the client leaves, his or her energy can still remain and you could bring the energy home.

As spiritual entrepreneurs, we put ourselves in the position of experiencing our clients' energy, which is part of the job. Yet it is not what our family, co-workers, or our next client has agreed to, so it is important to periodically clear both our physical bodies and our working space so that others are not affected by the energy of our clients.

There are many ways to release the energy of a client. Most modalities teach specific ways to do it, yet do we always remember to do it? Here are simple tips for clearing your energy and the energy in your workspace or home.

- Every time you leave or enter work, imagine that the doorframe is a car wash and as you walk through, all that is not for your highest and most loving energy is cleansed.
- Develop a ritual each time you finish with a client: release any unwanted energies to the light to be transformed into healing energy for your client.
- If you work in a store environment, quietly bless each person you see walking in the aisles, this helps raise the energy your clients give off.
- When you turn off the lights, do a quick Space Clearing Meditation (meditation is below).

- On your way home, spend some time in prayer asking that your energy, and the energy around you, reflects your highest spiritual intention.

You get the idea. Have some fun making up your own energy and space-clearing rituals.

It takes time to ingrain clearing energy in your routine, but soon you'll be clearing yourself and your space without a second thought. The following Space-Clearing Meditation works well for both your workplace and your home. Once mastered, you can do it very quickly, maybe in a minute or two. But at first, plan to take about 5 minutes.

SPACE-CLEARING MEDITATION

1. Take three deep breaths, and with each exhalation relax your shoulders further.
2. Return to breathing normally.
3. Now in your mind's eye, visualize the space you want to clear.
4. Imagine your entire space is filled with a bright golden light … as if there is a million-watt golden bulb, or a Divine Being, in the center.
5. See the light reaching every corner and crevice.
6. Envision yourself now standing outside of the space, seeing that beautiful, bright golden light coming out of all the windows and doors.
7. Imagine that the intensity and brightness is growing.
8. Ask that only the highest and most loving good be allowed to stay for the occupants of the space … and all that is not good, be removed and sent to the light for healing.
9. Ask that if any occupant, on a soul level, is not okay with the work that is being done today, that they will not be affected by the light work being done today.
10. We are intending that this cleansing is for the highest and most loving good of ALL that are involved.

This meditation is from *Soul Soothers: Mini Meditations for Busy Lives*, published by Findhorn Press. In this book you'll find more information about how you are affected by other people's energy and other mini meditations.

Afterword

• • • • • • • • • • • • • • •

LISA We are deeply honored to be with you on your journey to help others and raise the vibration of others on this planet. Just know that those you help will be grateful that you followed your guidance to be of service. Many people struggle to improve their lives and are looking for someone just like you for assistance. Because you took the steps to offer your services you can be there for them. I am grateful that you are building your spiritual business to help our human family. We need more people like you.

Cindy and I hope that we have given you the building blocks to grow your business and allow you to reach those who need you. Remember, if you are consistent, persistent and work at it, your spiritual business will grow and reach many. It does take time, but you will be rewarded with doing what you've been inspired to do and make a better world!

CINDY Lisa and I are honored to be a part of your journey toward owning a successful spiritual business. We have shared our knowledge, stories, and support with you. If I could share one more thing, it is to release judgment of what you feel you should accomplish in any given day. Self-judgment is a common condition for spiritual people and achieves nothing.

Wake up each day with gratitude that you are able to do the work you love, know that divine timing is often not on your timetable, and add a dash of humor and self-love to all you *do* get done each day. If you know you are doing the best you can in any given moment, the rest will take care of itself. Know it will never feel like your effort is enough, but it usually is. We are human beings and adjust your expectations accordingly.

We would love to hear feedback about your successes *and* your challenges. You can contact us through our websites, which you can find in Resources. We encourage you to join the growing number of spiritual businesses being of service and supporting their community, and through the ever-expanding Internet, serving the world.

Blessings,
Cindy Griffith and Lisa K., PhD

Resources

. . . .

EMAIL MARKETING SERVICES

- Mail Chimp
- Aweber
- Constant Contact
- iContact
- GetResponse
- Vertical Response
- Benchmark Email
- Mad Mimi

SOCIAL NETWORKING SERVICES

Please keep in mind social networking services come and go very quickly, it is best to do your own research on the current ones as you are researching what to use. The most popular ones as of the writing of this book are:

- Facebook
- Twitter
- YouTube
- Pinterest
- Google+
- LinkedIn
- Tumblr
- Instagram
- SnapChat
- MeetUp

RESOURCES FOR IMAGES AND PHOTOGRAPHS

Some sites charge for images. It is important to have permission to use any image.

- Fotolia.com
- POND5.com

- Shutterstock.com
- Resources for images and photographs you can get for free:
- freestockphotos.biz
- freedigitalphotos.net
- freepik.com
- unsplash.com

REFERENCE SOURCES FOR WHERE YOU CAN HIRE VIDEO AND WEBSITE FREELANCERS

- Elance.com
- Fiverr.com
- Freelance.com

AUTHOR'S WEBSITES

- GrowYourSpiritualBusinessBook.com – this book's website
- CindyGriffith.com – Cindy Griffith's website
- LMK88.com – Lisa K.'s website

RESOURCE DISCLAIMER: The resources listed here are intended for informational purposes only. The authors do not guarantee that the resource information is accurate, complete, reliable, current, and error-free or any other aspect with regards to this list. Inclusion or exclusion to this list should not be construed as an indication of approval, disapproval nor endorsement by the authors. No warranty of any kind is implied, nor will the authors assume any legal liability or responsibility for the content. We cannot guarantee the accuracy of the information posted on other sites.

Acknowledgments

· · · · · · · · · · · · · · · ·

CINDY GRIFFITH For me, this book's journey started at the Conscious Life Expo in Los Angeles. Our publicist, Gail Torr, saw how I was able to increase the booth sales for one of the attendees and suggested I write a book for spiritual business entrepreneurs. Soon after, I was on Lisa K.'s radio show and we found ourselves talking about our shared goal of writing a book to help people attain a successful spiritual business.

Lisa and I got together for lunch at a teashop in Westchester County and *Grow Your Spiritual Business* was born! We combined some of our ideas and brainstormed new ones. Lisa was amazing to work with and I cannot thank her enough for her wonderful ideas, patience, and easygoing style. Thank you, Lisa!

I also want to thank my husband, David Bennett who is the calm in my storm and my best friend and Mastermind buddy, Virginia "Kiki" Waldron for all their support. Lastly, I would like to thank all of the wonderful people at Findhorn Press. It seems to take a village to nurture a book and this one took the entire globe. From Scotland to France to the United States, everyone at Findhorn Press has been amazingly supportive and for that I am eternally grateful to be included in the Findhorn Press family of authors.

LISA K. My journey for this book started with many of my students and clients over the years asking me for advice on how to start their own spiritual business. To help them, I incorporated that advice into my *Developing Your Intuition Level 2* course for my advanced students. That material was so popular it eventually evolved into a course on its own called *How to Start Your Spiritual Business*. It was about that time that Cindy and I met when she was a guest on my radio show, Between Heaven and Earth.

We hit it off from the start and soon found ourselves talking over tea on collaboration for a book we both felt was very much needed. It was all history from there and through a wonderful working relationship with Cindy this book was born.

I want to thank you Cindy for our exciting brainstorming sessions, your ease of schedule juggling, hard work ethic, keeping things rolling, being so easy to get along with and making me laugh! We have an amazing "synergy" and I can't express in words how grateful I am for having you as my co-author.

I'd like to thank my wonderful family and most of all, my husband, Vincent, whose tremendous support, love and sage advice I couldn't live without in general but particularly in writing this book. Thank you Christopher for your expertise in English grammar. Thanks to my Mom and Dad for their undying belief in me in everything I do and their unconditional love that means the world to me.

Thank you to my wonderful friends and supporters. To my writers' group for the encouragement and positive feedback over the years: Maryse Godet Copans, Jane F. Collen, Ann Gulian and Mary O'Keefe Brady. To Stan Kogelman for your words of wisdom and counsel on being a book author. Jane, again thanks, for your expert advice in copyright law.

Finally thank you to Findhorn Press and all the wonderful people there for accepting me as one of their new authors. Thank you goes out to Gail Torr for encouraging me to write my own book long before this book was conceived, Sabine Weeke, and the others I've worked with at Findhorn Press who have all been so wonderful and kind to me.

About the Authors

· · · · · · · · · · · · · · · ·

CINDY GRIFFITH is an internationally renowned Psychic, Teacher, and Author, with a diverse background in Metaphysics, Meditation, Spiritual Development and Spiritual Business Counseling. She and her husband David Bennett have recently moved from the Finger Lake region of New York to Virginia Beach.

Cindy expresses her passions of teaching, writing and psychic counseling via clients and students in the USA and abroad. Recently she is teaching Spiritual and Psychic Development and offering channeled sessions in Tokyo, Japan.

In her private time, Cindy enjoys traveling; Sedona and the Dominican Republic are two of her favorite places, yet her spiritual sojourns to Egypt, Greece, Ireland, Australia and Italy have been amazing adventures! Her and David's book tours have knocked off bucket list items like driving through the Candelabra Tree as well as visiting Bryce and Antelope Canyon. Cindy also reads young adult series novels to soothe her inner child.

Holding both a Masters in Consciousness Development and a Bachelor of Science in Spiritual Counseling and Healing from SUNY Empire State, Cindy's a graduate of a three-year Metaphysical Teacher Training Program as well as taking her bodhisattva vows after three days of teaching from the Dalai Lama. Cindy graduated from Openway, a four-year energy healing school and is Reiki-certified.

Author of *Soul Soothers: Mini Meditations for Busy Lives* and two Meditation CDs: *Soul Soothers* and *Soul Expansion*, Cindy also co-authored *Voyage of Purpose* with her husband, David and now *Grow your Spiritual Business*, with Lisa K. PhD. She blogs for Huffington Post, Om Times, the Door Opener, her own WordPress blog and writes for spiritual magazines.

You can contact Cindy, read her Blogs, check her calendar, or simply learn more at CindyGriffith.com, discover about her and David's books at SpiritualSimplicityBooks.com and follow her on Facebook under Cindy Griffith's Giving Back Page.

LISA K., PHD, is a Teacher, Author and Speaker specializing in intuition. Through a global internet presence and in-person workshops, Lisa teaches others how to develop their intuition so they can make it happen when they want, on what they want and get detailed information. She has taught hundreds of people intuition development in workshops and seminars and is considered the intuition expert. Her public appearances reach people around the world through guest speaking, online media and her popular radio show, *Between Heaven and Earth*.

Lisa has run her spiritual business since 2007, nearly tripling her following in two years to over 13,000 through social media and direct marketing. She also teaches her business building techniques online, helping spiritual business entrepreneurs get their business started. As a keynote speaker, Lisa gives talks on intuition at health and wellness fairs, expos and other special events. As an author, Lisa's work is frequently published in a variety of widely distributed online magazines including Soul Essence, Inspire Me Today, Care2; she also is a Featured Columnist and spotlight writer for OmTimes Magazine.

In her earlier career, Lisa was a successful director, manager and project executive for fortune 500 companies in the US and Asia. Her leadership responsibilities spanned marketing, selling and delivering software and hardware solutions to large corporate industry leaders. Lisa has sold and led multi-million dollar information technology development projects for nationwide company infrastructures. Leading large teams of software developers, business analysts and systems engineers, Lisa and her teams implemented complex software systems for industries in retail banking, finance, medicine, shipping and technology.

Lisa holds degrees in Electrical Engineering from Columbia University, Psychobiology from the State University of New York, and a PhD in Metaphysical Sciences from the University of Metaphysical Sciences. Lisa is also certified in many energy healing and intuition modalities.

Lisa continues to practice and study Tai Chi Chuan, Bagua, Qi Gong and Wing Chun. She also volunteers her time as a member of local Board of Directors. Lisa and her family love to travel around the world, seeing new sights and learning about other cultures both ancient and contemporary. Lisa can be reached through her website at www.LMK88.com and via email contact@LMK88.com.

SOUL SOOTHERS

BY CINDY GRIFFITH

FEATURING ONE-PAGE MEDITATIONS that can be practiced all day—while doing the dishes, waiting at the doctor's office, or even in the shower—this book is designed to calm those with busy lives.

978-1-84409-608-4

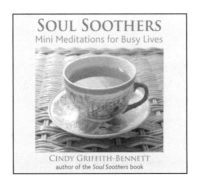

SOUL SOOTHERS MEDITATION CD

BY CINDY GRIFFITH

LEARN TO MEDITATE when your are at work, running errands, waiting in line, and even taking a shower!

978-1-84409-618-3

FINDHORN PRESS

Life-Changing Books

Consult our catalogue online
(with secure order facility) on
www.findhornpress.com

For information on the Findhorn Foundation:
www.findhorn.org

 **green press**
I N I T I A T I V E

FSC
www.fsc.org

MIX
Paper from
responsible sources
FSC® C013483